The Portrayal of Ann

Helenie Mende

The Portrayal of Anne Boleyn in "The Tudors"

Contemporariness in Historical Fiction

AV Akademikerverlag

Impressum/Imprint (nur für Deutschland/only for Germany)
Bibliografische Information der Deutschen Nationalbibliothek: Die Deutsche Nationalbibliothek verzeichnet diese Publikation in der Deutschen Nationalbibliografie; detaillierte bibliografische Daten sind im Internet über http://dnb.d-nb.de abrufbar.
Alle in diesem Buch genannten Marken und Produktnamen unterliegen warenzeichen-, marken- oder patentrechtlichem Schutz bzw. sind Warenzeichen oder eingetragene Warenzeichen der jeweiligen Inhaber. Die Wiedergabe von Marken, Produktnamen, Gebrauchsnamen, Handelsnamen, Warenbezeichnungen u.s.w. in diesem Werk berechtigt auch ohne besondere Kennzeichnung nicht zu der Annahme, dass solche Namen im Sinne der Warenzeichen- und Markenschutzgesetzgebung als frei zu betrachten wären und daher von jedermann benutzt werden dürften.

Coverbild: www.ingimage.com

Verlag: AV Akademikerverlag GmbH & Co. KG
Heinrich-Böcking-Str. 6-8, 66121 Saarbrücken, Deutschland
Telefon +49 681 9100-698, Telefax +49 681 9100-988
Email: info@akademikerverlag.de

Herstellung in Deutschland:
Schaltungsdienst Lange o.H.G., Berlin
Books on Demand GmbH, Norderstedt
Reha GmbH, Saarbrücken
Amazon Distribution GmbH, Leipzig
ISBN: 978-3-639-38511-3

Imprint (only for USA, GB)
Bibliographic information published by the Deutsche Nationalbibliothek: The Deutsche Nationalbibliothek lists this publication in the Deutsche Nationalbibliografie; detailed bibliographic data are available in the Internet at http://dnb.d-nb.de.
Any brand names and product names mentioned in this book are subject to trademark, brand or patent protection and are trademarks or registered trademarks of their respective holders. The use of brand names, product names, common names, trade names, product descriptions etc. even without a particular marking in this works is in no way to be construed to mean that such names may be regarded as unrestricted in respect of trademark and brand protection legislation and could thus be used by anyone.

Cover image: www.ingimage.com

Publisher: AV Akademikerverlag GmbH & Co. KG
Heinrich-Böcking-Str. 6-8, 66121 Saarbrücken, Germany
Phone +49 681 9100-698, Telefax +49 681 9100-988
Email: info@akademikerverlag.de

Printed in the U.S.A.
Printed in the U.K. by (see last page)
ISBN: 978-3-639-38511-3

Table of Contents

Introduction

"You think you know the story. But you only know how it ends. To get to the heart of the story, you have to go back to the beginning." These are the introductory lines of the opening credits of the historical television series *The Tudors*. These lines are spoken by the programme's central character Henry VIII., played by the Irish actor Jonathan Rhys Meyers. *The Tudors* was launched on the American cable network Showtime in April 2007, and is an Irish Canadian co-production that illustrates, as its title might already suggest, the life and reign a Tudor monarch, namely the infamous English King Henry Tudor, better known as Henry VIII. The show became commercially very successful so that the fourth and final season has only recently finished airing in the USA, ending with the death of Henry VIII. *The Tudors*' narrative structure has been arranged as follows: One episode has a duration of approximately fifty minutes, whereas one season consists of ten episodes, apart from the third season produced in 2009 with a total of only eight episodes. The first season sets out in the year 1518 when Henry is a young man in his late twenties and has been on the English throne for about a decade. This initial season ends with the portrayal of events of 1530, namely with the death of Cardinal Wolsey (Sam Neil) and Henry being in the middle of the proceedings to obtain an annulment for his marriage to Queen Katherine of Aragon (Maria Doyle Kennedy) in order to marry his mistress Anne Boleyn, played by Natalie Dormer. The time span of the subsequent season is a great deal shorter, only depicting events of four years time, that is from 1532 until 1536, climaxing in the execution of Henry's then second wife Anne Boleyn. Season three and four of *The Tudors* portray events from 1436 to the end of Henry VIII.'s reign. Unlike an historical film, which on average runs for about two hours, the serial format allows *The Tudors* to attempt a more expanded and more detailed filmic portrayal of Henry's life, with a total running time of thirty-two hours within these four seasons.

Henry's opening lines, however, have the function to inform the audience that this appropriation of sixteenth century English history will be different from most other previous depictions, and this not only with regard to its running time. There is of course a mythology surrounding Henry VIII.'s life, especially around his six marriages, and most appropriations rely on the awareness of that mythology. But Henry word's foreclose that awareness, indicating that nothing is as it may always have seemed. In doing so, Wray argues that *The Tudors* asks the viewer to discard preconception, whereas it emphasizes instead a new point of departure and innovative retracing procedure (40), and this it what distinguishes *The Tudors* from other portrayals of the Tudor dynasty.

Plainly speaking, *The Tudors* is historical fiction. Historical fiction is often lambasted by critics and historians for its historical inaccuracies, simplified storylines, fictionalizations and omissions. Toplin, however, has made the attempt to argue in defence of the portrayal of history on screen. Therefore, he has redefined this filmic genre, renaming it cinematic history, which includes any portrayal that brings the past to life on screen. He believes that cinematic history should not merely be dismissed as fiction, as, within the medium of film, it can offer a valid reinterpretations of history (1-7). In this regard, also *The Tudors* offers a valid reinterpretation of history, albeit in an innovative way, as Henry heralds in the opening.

It has to be noted, however, that cinematic history primarily refers to feature films, regardless of whether shown on television or in the cinema. Nevertheless, Toplin does not explicitly exclude television series from the genre since its main trait is that it references dramatic illustrations of the past, which are aimed at mass audiences (3). Thus, it can be argued that, although *The Tudors* is not a film, but a television series, it nevertheless qualifies as cinematic history, as it portrays the past and is targeted at the mass-market.

Toplin has defined several characteristics for the genre of cinematic history, and most of them are partly as well as entirely applicable to *The Tudors*.[1] One characteristic is particularly significant within the scope of this thesis, that is that cinematic history speaks to the present. When interpreting the past, cinematic history references the present, with the objective to attempt to establish a modern-day relevance for the viewer. The present is always manifest in historical films and programmes. Hence, regardless how historically accurate a film might be in its depiction and reinterpretation of history, a certain spirit of contemporariness is always perceptible (41-46). At the same time, a feeling for the past is communicated through the film-makers' attention given to details of an earlier age (Toplin 47). Thus, by doing so, historical fiction, or cinematic history, conveys an interconnectedness of period detail and contemporariness, which is also materialized in *The Tudors*. This is necessary to reach the mainstream audience. While a sense of the "pastness of the past" is mediated (Toplin 48), which gives the audience the opportunity to travel into a foreign land called the (imagined) past, the viewer still has to be able to identify with and/or relate to the historical characters and happenings. And this can, amongst other things, be achieved by interpreting the past with a modern sensibility. And this is exactly what distinguishes *The Tudors* from many other filmic reinterpretations of Henry VIII.'s court. The series offers a very modernized depiction that abandons the popular image that people have of Henry VIII. as the obese tyrant who liked to discard and

---

1 Please see pages 8-57 for Toplin's elaborate account of the characteristics of cinematic history including examples.

even kill his numerous wives.

Another issue, which is important to be mentioned within the context of historical fiction, the mass-market and *The Tudors*, is entertainment. As already stated, history on screen is often subject to criticism for being portrayed too simplified, historically inaccurate, etc. What often seems to be ignored is the fact that, unlike history documentaries, which are generally watched by a more sophisticated audience, historical fiction films or television programmes have the primary agenda to entertain a mass audience. Educational purposes are secondary, which does not necessarily mean that the quality has to suffer. *The Tudors* has also been subject to stark criticism for its too modernized portrayal and its alleged historical inaccuracy. A BBC spokeswoman[2] has stated in defense of the show that "*The Tudors* is not a a drama documentary [...] It is a highly authored and entertaining interpretation of events during a period of history" (Martin). Most films and television programmes, historical or not, want to reach as great an audience as possible, regardless of age, social background, gender and race, and are therefore adapted to mainstream interests. But what is even of greater significance is that history on screen is an entirely different medium as history on the written page, thus, different rules apply. In contrast to books, film is a very visual medium. It conveys more than just a collection facts; it allows history to be a performance, a work that constructs and stages the past in sound and images (Rosenstone 1-10). And within the leeway of these means of representing history, cinematic history can achieve something that history books cannot, that is to allow contemporariness to flow into an illustration of pastness. Thus, the present and the past close ranks. *The Tudors* is exemplary of that. Especially, where the character of Anne Boleyn is concerned.

Within its generally rather modernized reinvention of Tudor history, it is particularly *The Tudors*' Anne Boleyn who is represented in contemporary terms. The objective of this thesis therefore is to focus on the portrayal of Anne Boleyn in *The Tudors* in general, whereas within this analysis, the primary focus will be put on the argument that Dormer depicts a very contemporized Anne Boleyn, which has the effect that she seems to have a great appeal to modern-day audiences. The means of recreating a historical figure in a historical television series (or film) in a contemporary way are manifold. With regard to Anne Boleyn in *The Tudors*, this research shall be concerned with the following: physical appearance in the sense of casting Anne Boleyn, representation of female behaviour and the mediality of costume.

---

2 The show has also been broadcast to British audiences by the BBC.

As Anne Boleyn is executed in the last episode of the second season of *The Tudors*, this thesis shall only be concerned with season one and season two of the series. Scenes, still photographs and images of the programme will be used for interpretations and analyses in order to determine manifestations of contemporary spirit interlaced into the period detail of historical appropriations. As there has been made only one academic publications about *The Tudors* as a topic of research to this point, that is by Ramona Wray, both the argumentations and the according examples of the thesis will be suggestive, and generally the approach will be in many ways more practical than theoretical. The main sources of information about the television programme have usually been newspaper articles and reviews. Also both Showtime's website about the series and the *Tudors Wiki* often provided useful material such a interviews with the actors and the writer of show, Michael Hirst, images and useful comments. Furthermore, various works on the field of representing history on screen or film studies in general have been used for reference, as well as a number of monographs on Tudor England, the Tudor court and its habits and customs, on Henry VIII. and his six wives, in order to compare how the written historical sources have been both used and ignored to reinvent the Henrican court on screen, always with the focus on contemporariness, as the thesis will not be concerned with how accurately history is turned into fiction.

Before this thesis will, however, treat the different means to achieve a contemporary portrayal of Anne Boleyn, the first chapter will be concerned with a general approach to *The Tudors*. A short summary will be given about the previous filmic rewritings of Tudor history, including films about Anne Boleyn, establishing the idea that the Tudor monarchs and the people who had an impact on them are popular subjects within historical appropriations. In this context, the initial chapter strives to unveil the reasons and motives for the universal appeal of Renaissance history rewritings, particularly in our current age. With a brief focus on Rhys Meyers' portrayal of Henry VIII. in *The Tudors*, a link between cultural iconography and the modern-day fascination with celebrity will be established. Furthermore, it will be argued that the two most important Tudor monarchs Henry VIII. and Elizabeth I still hold a certain prominence in the contemporary mind, with the attempt to build a connection to Anne Boleyn. This chapter will then be concluded by again picking up the idea that *The Tudors* is unique in the way it portrays the Henrican court, hinting at Dormer's Anne Boleyn, who will be the focal point of the subsequent chapters.

That in historical fiction the characters depicted are often reinterpreted in contemporary terms is made clear by *The Tudors'* portrayal of Anne Boleyn. Dormer's Anne Boleyn is one of the characters in *The Tudors* where this premise is realized not just

6

marginally but to a great extent. Therefore, chapter two will focus on the character's sheer physicality arguing that a great part of the contemporariness of Dormer's Anne Boleyn is founded in her beauty and attractiveness, which is an important element in mainstream American television shows and films. How this is reconcilable with what is known about the historical Anne Boleyn's appearance will also be considered. Additionally, in that context, also Rhys Meyer's Henry will be briefly regarded as he appears to look like "a very different Henry from the king immortalised in Hans Holbein's portraits," as remarked by Sherwin.

Also the show's depiction of Anne's personality, general behaviour and conduct often seems rather influenced by contemporary standards, an aspect that will be extensively dealt with in the third chapter. Therefore, the sixteenth century definitions of femininity will be briefly summarized and contrasted to how Anne is portrayed in *The Tudors*. In that context, it will be argued that Anne is re-imagined as a pawn in her father's and uncle's game to secure the family's power and fortune, a subdued female who has no other choice but to obey due the prevailing patriarchal structures. These restricting circumstances are, however, dissolved as Anne increasingly gains power. A point which is deployed to reconstruct Anne as a strong-willed and smart woman, perfectly suitable for a post-feminist audience. Her importance is furthermore stressed when she is later illustrated as a key-reforming figure, as will also be proved in this chapter. Generally, it will be claimed that *The Tudors* offers a very sympathetic portrayal of Anne Boleyn since she is re-imagined as both a victim and the tragic heroine of a male-dominated Tudor world.

While analysing both scenes and still images of *The Tudors*, the fourth chapter shall then be concerned with the mediality of costume, demonstrating that Anne Boleyn's seemingly historical costumes are rather influenced by contemporary ideas of fashion since *The Tudors*' costume designer intentionally reinterpreted the costumes in modern terms to visually build a bridge from the past to the present. Additionally, aspects of authentic Tudor clothing will be considered and compared to their realization on the programme. That costumes are furthermore important for communicating a certain image or purpose will be proved in the analysis of the show's intention to reflect Anne's social rise in the evolution of her dresses, whereas historical accuracy is not essentially necessary for this aspect.

As this thesis is generally concerned with the contemporariness of Anne Boleyn's character in *The Tudors*, it might be worth attempting to evoke associations between Anne Boleyn and contemporary women, both real and fictional. Natalie Dormer has for instance stated that she sees Anne Boleyn as a Lady Diana Spencer of the Tudor times, a

7

statement that shall be considered and interpreted here. Furthermore, the real and the fictional Anne Boleyn will be established as a fashion-icon here, which will not only link her to Princess Diana but also to Carrie Bradshaw, the central character of the series *Sex and the City*. By comparing Anne Boleyn to contemporary women, this final chapter attempts to intensify its previous argumentations that the portrayal of Anne Boleyn in *The Tudors*, where her beauty, behaviour and costume is concerned, is utterly influenced by contemporary standards and therefore offers a highly modernized interpretation of Henry VIII.'s second wife.

1. The Importance of Being Tudor: Rewriting Tudor History On Screen

Before attempting to analyse the portrayal of the character of Anne Boleyn in *The Tudors*, it is worth ascertaining why Tudor history seems to have such an appeal to audiences. Ever since film making started over a hundred years ago, the Tudors have been a popular subject for motion pictures. One of the first silent short-films ever made was called *The Execution of Mary Stuart*, depicting in about twenty seconds the titled historical event. This film was produced by Thomas Edison in 1895, and even though it technically deals with a Stuart monarch, it qualifies as Tudor cinema as Mary Stuart is the grand-daughter of Henry VIII. sister Margaret Tudor and whose execution is founded in the quarrel between her and her cousin Elizabeth Tudor about the claim to the English throne. Ever since this very first filmic account, though very short it may have been, more than fifty films and/or television shows starring the Tudor dynasty have been produced.[3] Almost twenty of these films or series deal with Queen Elizabeth I. Unsurprisingly, she is the Tudor monarch who is most featured on screen, followed by her father Henry VIII. with about ten portrayals. Third positioned is the already mentioned Scottish Queen Mary Stuart, with six filmic accounts about her ill-fated life. The other films centre on Henry VIII.'s son Edward, Lady Jane Grey, Mary Tudor and Charles Brandon. One film has respectively been done on Henry VII., Sir Thomas More and William Tyndale even. What is striking is that only one of Henry VIII's six wives has had made films about her life as the eponymous heroine: that is Anne Boleyn. Of course, Henry's other wives appear in numerous Tudor films, such as *The Six Wives of Henry VIII* (1970) or *The Private Life of Henry VIII* (1933), yet not as the main female lead but as supporting characters. Anne Boleyn, on the other hand, has had five films produced, first and foremost centring on her life, not merely as one of Henry's wives. The first film about Anne Boleyn dates back as early as 1913, a French silent film, simply called *Anne de Boleyn*. A few years later, in 1920, the German silent film *Anna Boleyn* was produced. And then it took almost half a century before Anne Boleyn would star another film as the main character. In 1969 Geneviève Bujold plays Anne in Charles Jarrott's *Anne of the Thousand Days*. Contemporary portrayals on screen about Anne Boleyn's life are to be found in two adaptations of Philippa Gregory's novel *The Other Boleyn Girl* (2002): one produced in 2003 for the BBC, and the other one in 2007 as a big Hollywood blockbuster, starring Natalie Portman as Henry's second wife and Scarlett Johansson as her sister Mary Boleyn. Last but not least, *The Tudors* can also join the list of filmic depictions centring on Anne Boleyn, as she plays the leading female role in the first two seasons. To

---

3 A complete list of all films and television shows about the Tudor dynasty can be found on http://tudorhistory.org.

9

sum up, Anne Boleyn is without doubt the most famous of Henry's wives and that is the reason why she has already been a popular historical character to be portrayed when film was still in its infancy in the early 1900s, in the late sixties and she is especially popular now in the 2000s. Generally, one can say that the Tudors have been put on celluloid continuously in every decade since the 1900s, but it seems that the decade of 2000 to 2010 has brought forward slightly more Tudor films than the previous decades, as for instance *Elizabeth: The Golden Age* (directed by Shekhar Kapur 2007), *Henry VIII* (directed by Pete Travis, 2003), *The Twisted Tale of Bloody Mary* (directed by Chris Barnard, 2008) etc.[4] Surely, Anne Boleyn seems to have profited from that tendency.

There are various reasons why the Tudor family has been prominent on film especially in the last decade. Similar to Toplin, Sanders argues that often a specific historical event is illustrated and displayed on screen for two reasons: one, its own literary and imaginative content is considered so extremely rich and significant that audiences need to be enlightened about it; and two, that there are parallels and comparisons with contemporary or topical issues which can be evoked; history is, so to say, put in contemporary context (138-39). Without doubt, the first reason is liable to a certain subjectivity since it is hard to determine which historical event has been exciting enough to be worth to be picturized. With regard to the popularity of Tudor history in the last decade, the second reason, however, has a less subjective validation. There have been two important anniversaries with regard to Tudor history. First, in 2003 it was the four-hundredth anniversary of Queen Elizabeth I.'s death. And in 2009 the five-hundredths anniversary of Henry VIII.'s accession to the English throne was celebrated. In honour of this historically significant important happening of June 24, 1409, a great number of special exhibitions and events took place in Great Britain throughout the year, as for instance exhibitions in the National Portrait Gallery in London, called *Henry VIII Remembered*, or one with the apt title *Dressed to Kill* in The Tower of London. Also, lectures by Tudor historians and even a Tudor Music Festival at Hampton Court were held.[5] Interestingly, also a Facebook page named "Henry VIII 2009 Events" has been created. Facebook, belonging to the relatively new type of media, the social media, is an expression of a very modern trend, and the fact that a king who ruled half a century ago has his own page on it is again an instance where history meets modernity. In general, this also proves that Tudor monarchs like Elizabeth I. and Henry VIII. still play an important role

---

4 Information, such as year of release or name of the director etc., of the films mentioned has been taken from the Internet Movie Database.
5 A calendar of events and exhibitions in celebration of the 500th anniversary of Henry VIII's accession to the throne can be found on http://www.tudorhistory.org/files/henry500.html

in contemporary Britain. They are still remembered for their achievements and have a certain presence in the British mind. This becomes obvious in the survey conducted by the BBC in 2002. Here thirty-thousand British people were asked via internet or telephone, who they consider to be the greatest Briton of all time. Queen Elizabeth I. is ranked number seven and is the only monarch who secured herself a position in the top ten of the list of the hundred greatest Britons of all time. Henry VIII. is ranked on number forty. In total, there are eleven British monarchs on the list whereas Elizabeth I. and Henry VIII. are the only ones from the Tudor dynasty. Evaluating the results of the list, the BBC has stated that analysts argue that, as no person in the top ten is still alive (for instance Winston Churchill, Lady Diana, William Shakespeare, Charles Darwin), British people do not have that great an obsession with current celebrity as it may sometimes seem. Historically important people like Henry and Elizabeth Tudor have manifested themselves as cultural icons, and the fact that they are no longer alive has turned them into legends and myths. In our contemporary society, people are fascinated by celebrities, even though that fascination is not as great as it may at first appear, as already been mentioned. But what happens if one combines the fascination with current celebrity with the fascination of cultural icons of an earlier period? The answer is a production of an historical film about such an icon and with a cast of famous actors the general public is interested in. Or one casts an yet unknown actor/actress as a significant historical figure and, in doing so, contributes to their status of celebrity. Regardless of whether this has been realized intentionally or not, both these instances are exemplary in *The Tudors*. When Rhys Meyers had been cast as Henry VIII. for the series, he had already been an acclaimed actor and model. Wray even argues that there is a certain intertexuality in Rhys Meyers playing the role of Henry, as he already has the reputation of portraying enigmatic and disturbing parts in films such as *Matchpoint* (directed by Woody Allen, 2005) and *Titus* (directed by Julie Taymor, 2000). Furthermore, he already has had the experience to play a king who is also haunted by fear of ageing, sleeplessness and hypochondria, that is the 'King of Rock 'n Roll' in the CBS mini series *Elvis* (2005), for whose portrayal he has even won a Golden Globe. Another intertextual connection between Ryhs Meyers and Henry VIII. is the actor's troubled celebrity status, which is often publicized in the media. The stereotype of the hard-living Irish actor, who had a difficult Irish childhood, functions to romanticize Rhys Meyers' own drinking problems that are often laid bare in the tabloids (44-45), as for example only lately, when Rhys Meyers was too intoxicated with alcohol to board a flight of United Airlines. He was then barred from the flight whereupon the actor verbally offended the staff and is now banned for life from flying with the airline. A few weeks earlier, he had already even been arrested for attacking the staff of a bar at a Paris airport, threatening to kill them, as reported by the *Daily Mail*.

With regard to Irishness, it is argued that the "whiff of alcoholic drink" combined with Rhys Meyers "bad boy" image works to invest the character of Henry with a fascinating unpredictability, as opposed to the very often predictable acting abilities of various non-Irish Hollywood stars (Wray 45). As a cultural icon, people do not only think of Henry VIII. as playing a major role in the English Reformation, they also see him as an choleric, unpredictable monster he became in his later years. So both Rhys Meyers' and Henry's unpredictability, manifested in outbursts of fury, is something these two men have in common. As a result, this intertexuality works as a direct link between the fascination with the contemporary celebrity of Rhys Meyers and iconography of the historical figure of King Henry VIII.

So both Elizabeth I. and Henry VIII. are two English monarchs that still claim a certain prominence in the contemporary (British) mind, even though they reigned half a millennia ago. But with regard to Anne Boleyn, what may be the reason for her newly found presence on screen in the 2000s? As already mentioned, she is the only one of Henry's six wives about whom entire films have been made. She has also inspired numerous plays, operas and biographies since her story can be considered as one of the greatest dramas ever taken place in the history of England, with all the necessary dramatic elements such as ill-stared love, power, glory, lust and of course a tragic ending (Richardson 60). Due to the respective anniversaries of Henry VIII. and Elizabeth I., Tudor history currently seems to present a high marketability, and Anne Boleyn plays a great role in that since she is Elizabeth's mother and next to Henry VIII. the other parent to one of the greatest queens ever to rule England. So this makes out an interesting family triangle consisting of a simple nuclear family of mother-father-child, a triangle that is certainly not disregarded in *The Tudors*. This triangle, however, is not so simple with regard to both the family drama that happened within it and of course the family's royal status. Nowadays, a divorce is nothing unusual. Mothers are bringing up their children alone and fathers are leaving their families. A general instability in family life has never been greater than in our contemporary Western society. It can be argued that this is the reason why the portrayal of the Tudor family drama has a great appeal to contemporary audiences, according to the principle what is just a simple divorce in comparison to a divorce followed by an execution by one's ex-husband? In that case, Toplin's argument that in cinematic history the past speaks to the present is applicable. It can be suggested that the current familial instabilities are mirrored in Henry's own familial instabilities.

12

But it is not solely the family drama of the Tudor dynasty that presents such a high marketability. Bearing in mind that *The Tudors* has been made for an American audience, it is necessary to mention that the Renaissance is especially for American viewers the great era of prosperity, power and sensuality, as is argued in a German history magazine. From a European perspective, it is particularly the Italian sovereigns of the Renaissance period that were known for their excessive lifestyle and absolutism. But in the USA, this seems typical of entire Renaissance Europe, including England (Engelmann). Thus, the rewriting of Tudor history in the American popular media must necessarily be a lavish and glorious one. For that purpose, no medium is better suited than film or television.

For Jurkiewitz, a professor at Central Michigan University, the argument why the early modern era generally appeals to modern sensibility, is that this period was characterized by a very complex scheming, superficially hidden by a calm and serene formality, which certainly was instrumental in provoking an unbelievable sense of insecurity. An insecurity that is also noticeable in our own time (La Ferla). *The Tudors'* writer Michael Hirst believes that historical material needs to reflect the contemporary viewer in some way and that its themes have to be compatible with one's own life in order to be interesting to an audience. As a result, with an emphasis on the personal and human core of its protagonists, *The Tudors* depicts, in a language that is a juxtaposition between authentic Tudor speech, diligently extracted of genuine Tudor documents by researchers, and current slang (Fletcher), historical events that have shaped the history of Britain as well as of America forever (*Good to Be King* xi-xii), thus building a bridge to the present. It is tempting to ponder how the English Reformation, or if at all, would have taken place if Anne Boleyn had not crossed Henry VIII.'s path. Which consequences would this have had in the context of the establishment of the Anglican Church and the English settlements in the New World? In that regard, their fateful encounter, and the love story that comes with it, is utterly fascinating. In the long run, it changed England from Catholicism to Protestantism, which did not only have an impact on European history but also on American history. Herrup goes as far as to even argue that although "as Americans accepted the conflicted diversity of [their] beginnings, the Anglophile's dream of lineal descent from a heroic Elizabethan age survived." Nevertheless, Semenza concedes that one has to be careful trying to find reasons why the Renaissance seems such a popular period to be reproduced on screen as this interest can be explained in the general proliferation of the popular culture industry itself. Although in the years between 1935 and 1944 at least four major films depicted the Renaissance as a historical source from which, in a time of international crisis, one could draw national pride, inspiration and moral

13

influence, it has to be acknowledged that not all cinematic portrayals of the Tudor era are politically motivated (1-2). Bearing this in mind, one has to consider *The Tudors*. There is no real political or ideological motivation behind this series. Its main purpose is to entertain and to show that people like Anne Boleyn or Henry VIII. are not simply museum pieces of an era long gone but that they were also human beings who suffered, loved, died and had a variety of feelings, just like everyone else (Hirst interviewed by Gomeshi). As a result, *The Tudors* is different than any other filmic depictions of the eponymous dynasty (Herrup). In that context, Herrup claims that "what *The Tudors* distinguishes is its soap opera style – more explicitly sexual, more embedded in modern popular culture (especially via advertising), and more assertive in its conflation of past and present," which will be more clearly demonstrated in the following chapters by analysing means of portraying the character of Anne Boleyn in *The Tudors*.

2. Beauty Is in the The Eye of the Beholder: Natalie Dormer as Anne Boleyn

In the previous chapter, it has been suggestively argued that in order to link the contemporary obsession with celebrity with interest in cultural icons both popular and yet unknown actors/actresses are cast as such in historical films or television programmes. Although Anne Boleyn is not invested with the same overwhelming iconographic status as Henry VIII. or their daughter Elizabeth, she nevertheless, it can be suggested, is an important historical figure that the people are fascinated with. The actress, Natalie Dormer, who was chosen to play Anne Boleyn in *The Tudors* had until then been relatively unknown, but her portrayal of Anne Boleyn certainly has stirred an interest in both herself and the character she is playing.

As a matter of fact, Henry's opening words are also applicable to the general representation of Anne Boleyn in *The Tudors*. Similar to the common preconception of Henry VIII. as a fat wife-killer, Anne Boleyn is often prejudiced as the other woman who consciously schemed to usurp Katherine of Aragon's place as the Queen of England. But as Henry instructs the viewer "to go back to the beginning," both Henry's and Anne's images in the popular mind are redefined. As a result ,Dormer's Anne Boleyn, it may be argued, is very different from that of other previous actresses. Formally, this difference is of course due to the extent of her filmic depiction over two seasons, which equals about fifteen hours of running time. But it is her very much contemporized depiction that is most noticeable. Plainly spoken, this already begins with Dormers physical appearance, for, as it will be argued, she corresponds to the contemporary ideal of beauty, which is often necessary for mainstream television series or films.

To begin with, in order to demonstrate how modern the show's approach to Renaissance history is and how much it is embedded in popular culture, as Herrup as argued, a comparative interpretation of four selected images is necessary.[6] Image 01 is a promotional shot for the second season of *The Tudors* showing Jonathan Rhys Meyers as Henry VIII. standing behind Natalie Dormer as Anne Boleyn. In this full body shot, in a possessive stature Henry has wrapped his right arm around Anne's waist, his left hand holding on to her neck. With her left hand Anne seductively touches her collar bone while her right hand holds a golden cup filled with red wine, which she is spilling in that very moment. Anne is wearing a shoulder-free, slim-fitting champaign coloured silk dress, partly see-through, which resembles a modern day lingerie-inspired nightdress. Apart from the dress, Anne also wears jewellery such as a flower-shaped gold ring on her left index finger,

---

6 Please see illustrations at the end of the paper.

a necklace with a cross pendant as well as silver earrings and a gemmed crown-like headband that holds back her dark brown hair which she wears down. She seductively gazes into the camera with bedroom eyes and her blood red lips slightly opened. As Henry is mostly covered by Anne's body, one can only see his upper body and head. He is wearing a black sleeveless waistcoat, hung with pompous silver chains, which works to accentuate his muscular arms. His dark hair is sleekly combed back, the beard above his upper lip and on his chin is cleanly shaven, his intense and powerful gaze mesmerising the observer. The brownish, ornamented background is less spectacular than the image's main occupants. A vase with two white roses is standing on a little table next to the royal couple. What becomes immediately obvious with this photograph is that it does not correspond at all to the image that people would have in mind of a king and his queen in the sixteenth century, let alone the iconographic Holbein-image of Henry VIII. Transmitting catchwords like seduction, beauty, sex, power and royalty, this representation of Anne and Henry does not fall short at all in its function as a promotional shot in its primary objective to obtain the attention of a mass audience. Furthermore, Henry symbolically grabbing Anne's neck while she spills red wine resembling her own blood foregrounds her tragic fate which is certainly oddly fascinating for contemporary audiences as it seems implausible that a man would have his wife executed. On the whole, apart from perhaps Henry's waistcoat, Anne's headband, the old-fashioned wall paper in the background and the seemingly darker lightening conditions, which all attempt to hint at some sort of feeling of pastness, this probably digitally enhanced photograph (if one looks for example at the unnatural smoothness of their skin) of The Tudors' Anne and Henry seems extremely modernized, and if one compares this image to the following image 02 this case in point may be made. Image 02 is a fashion shot from the Hugo Boss mainline from the spring and summer collection 2008. Even though this photo is an upper body close-up as opposed to the full-body shot of image 01 and the two comparing images were respectively shot for different occasions, they bear a number of similarities. To begin with, both couples appeal to contemporary ideals of beauty and attractiveness with regard to their faces and bodies. Although image 01 portrays two characters of a television programme or an actress and an actor, both could as easily be photo models as the unknown man and woman from the fashion advertisement. In respect of this, it is worth emphasizing that Rhys Meyers has worked as a model, both previous and simultaneous to his acting career, whereas he has also even featured a fashion campaign of the previously mentioned designer label. Furthermore, both couples strike a similar pose. Like Henry, the male model stands behind the female holding her neck with his left hand. His gaze is as engaging as Henry's and both wear their hair in the same fashion. Unlike Anne, the female model has her body slightly turned to the male model and does not directly look into the camera. Nevertheless, she also looks very seductive with her ruby red lips. She, too, has her left arm lifted but not to touch her collar bone but to draw attention to her white handbag, as the shot still functions as advertisement. The couple of image 02 are respectively wearing expensive watches and although different in style, they do not fail to keep up with the (imagined) royal couple's jewellery. Image 02 seems to have been shot under almost natural lightening conditions somewhere in the nature, as the treetops and the blue sky reveal, thus entirely different from the brownish wallpaper of *The Tudors*' promotional shot. To conclude this initial comparative study, it is striking that even though different in some instances, the image of Anne and Henry can manage to compare to a contemporary advertisement of a popular twenty-first century designer label. Clearly, image 01 displays some minor historical elements to emphasize the show's genre as a historical television series, but it can be argued that the image bears a greater resemblance to modern-day fashion advertisements, which can be found in all sorts of contemporary magazines, than to a credible photographic attempt to re-imagine what Henry VIII. and Anne Boleyn would actually have looked or posed like if photography had already existed in the sixteenth century. Like image 02 has the function to encourage people to buy designer items, image 01 animates people to become interested in the show, which certainly would not work if the promotional image was old-fashioned and uninviting.

To emphasize once more the link between contemporary obsession with celebrity and cultural icons within the context of how Anne (and Henry) are portrayed in *The Tudors*, a comparison of two more photographs is necessary. If one takes a look at images 03 and 04, it becomes immediately clear, what a great deal of similarity they are bearing. Image 03 is again a promotional shot from the second season of *The Tudors*. A contrast between image 01 and 03 is noticeable. In spite of both images being shot in order to promote the second season of the show, they differ slightly. They again both communicate the same catchwords, but image 03 seems to have put more emphasis on its historical realization where costume and décor are concerned. The brown floor with its rhombus-shaped pattern, the green satin curtain in the background, Anne's pompous robe, Henry's garment and the noble piece of furniture all create a sense of pastness in the image, even though not everything is accurately sixteenths century adapted, as for instance the divan where the royal couple is lying on did not exist as a type of sofa at that time. This piece of furniture became fashionable in Europe only in the nineteenth century,[7] but this is not significant as it still creates an image of pastness. On the whole, the photograph does not seem contemporized to the same extent as the other promotional shot. Still, it is greatly influenced by modern standards of advertising and promotion as further contrasting will reveal. Looking at image 04, the respective couples' poses are almost identical, with the exception that in image 04 the woman is situated on top of the man. In image 03, the opposite is the case, which might suggest that in *The Tudors* the male will dominate the female, as is expected from historical narratives about times where the term feminism did not even exist. Image 04, however, as a modern-day fashion advertisement allows the female to dominate the male and thus represents shifted gender relations of the twenty-first century.

Most people who are familiar with our temporary popular culture will be able to identify the models of image 04. They are Victoria and David Beckham, in the tabloid press also often referred to as Becks and Posh. This photograph is an underwear advertising campaign of the designer label Georgio Armani, which uses the celebrity status of the Beckhams to advertise their products on a greater scale. David and Victoria Beckham are both appearing frequently in the English tabloid press (meanwhile also in the USA) and they are a perfect example for our modern society's fascination with stardom. Contrasting these two images of a representation of the King of England and his wife, and the King of English Football and his former pop-singer wife has the purpose to demonstrate how much *The Tudors* incorporates a certain contemporariness into its historical matter. As in image 01 and 02, the couples represent the same sexiness, beauty and attractiveness that appeals to our modern eye and which film, television and advertising is unimaginable to do without. These two promotional shots of Anne and Henry promise the audience a very modern approach to sixteenths century English history. The programme certainly will be "a version of the Tudors for people who are used to watching contemporary TV" (Leith), so what the series accordingly needs is thrilling storylines, a network of intrigues, a great deal of love, romance and sex and of course attractive and fascinating actors and actresses, which the promotional photographs have already stipulated.

So with respect to that, the character of Anne Boleyn in *The Tudors* needs to be portrayed, above all, as a beautiful, desirable and seductive young woman. But how did the real Anne Boleyn look like, how or to which extent is that realized in *The Tudors*' episodes and does her actual appearance even have to matter for a filmic portrayal? By

---

7 For further information on the subject see Edward Lucie-Smith, *Furniture – A Concise History* (London. Thames and Hudson, 1979).

her contemporaries, such as the French courtier Brantôme, Anne Boleyn was described as "the fairest and most bewitching of all the lovely dames of the French court" (Weir 151). That description derives from the time she served the French Queen Claude, as a young woman, at court in France before coming to the English court. There, also the King of France, Francis I., was utterly fascinated by Anne and even wrote about her: "Venus était blonde, on m'a dit: L'on voit bien, qu'elle est brunette" (Weir 151). These descriptions of her certainly are extremely flattering but in how far they were subject to male courteous conduct is not determinable. It was, however, noted that Anne's apparent charm was not entirely founded in her looks but also in her gracefulness, her vibrant character and her quick wit. Her physique was rather petite that made her seem fragile, which appealed greatly to the male courtiers. Anne Boleyn had very long dark brown hair, but it was said that what was most attractive about her were her dark, almost black eyes, and Anne was certainly aware of the mesmerising effect they had on a number of men. Nevertheless, it has been remarked that Anne was not overly beautiful in the conventional sense and her physical appearance did not conform to the ideals of beauty of Early Modern England. In her time, it was fashionable for women to have a voluptuous figure and pale skin. Anne had neither. She had a very slender frame with small breasts and her complexion was of a darker colour. Anne also had some little physical imperfections. She had tiny moles on her skin, an unfemininely large Adam's apple and a second nail upon the side of one of her fingernails, which she felt self-conscious about. Nonetheless, Henry VIII.'s second wife was considerable pretty, a good dancer, eloquent, charming, even amusing but supposedly not as arrestingly attractive as Henry's former mistress Elizabeth Blount. However, Anne Boleyn did have a fascinating personality and another unexplainable quality, that is her sex appeal. Additionally, due to to her dark hair, black eyes and dark complexion, she seemed extremely exotic. Those are the reasons why so many men were infatuated by her. She was not a beauty in a conventional way, but she made men believe that she was (Weir 151-152).

But there are also some written accounts in which she has been described "as ugly, hideously deformed by a huge wen hidden by high-necked gowns, and a sixth finger on one hand" (Lindsey 47), although most of these unflattering descriptions of Anne Boleyn appeared in the decades after her execution when the collective memory of her was still shaped by her condemnation for witchcraft, adultery and incest, thus their validity remains doubtful. At the Tudor court it was fashionable to wear low-necked gowns; hence it would not have been possible for Anne to have hidden a wen on her neck. Also it is questionable that the King of England would have felt attracted to a woman who had a sixth finger

(Lindsey 47).

Whether deformed, hideous, exotically beautiful or fascinating, as the medium of photography unfortunately did not yet exist in the sixteenth century, the only clues to Anne Boleyn's physical appearance can be drawn from the surviving portraits of her, whereas portraits can also be very inaccurate, as Holbein's portrait of Henry VIII.'s fourth wife Anne of Cleves and the distress this evoked in Henry has demonstrated. There are, however, several portraits of Anne Boleyn existing. Image 05 and 06 show two of them. Image 05 is a portrait of Anne Boleyn by an unknown artist, deriving from an earlier version, and is to be found in Hever Castle in Kent, the Boleyn's former family residence. In the top left corner it says 'ang regina', Latin for 'Queen of England', so it can be presumed that the original version was painted some time during her reign as queen consort, so between 1533 and 1536. That is also the case for the portrait of Anne by an unknown artist in image 06. It, too, is a copy of an earlier version of a portrait of hers from the time of her reign and is currently displayed in the National Portrait Gallery in London.[8] Images 05 and 06 show, as most portraits in which the sitter is claimed to be Anne Boleyn, a woman with a long, thin but delicate face, dark hair and piercing dark eyes, a pointy chin, a small mouth with narrow reddish lips and high cheekbones. The Hever Castle portrait shows a very exotic and beautiful looking Anne. She wears a black low-necked dress, a French hood bedecked with pearls and a matching pearl necklace with a "B" pendant referring to her family name. Anne loved initial pendants and possessed at least two others with an 'A' and an 'AB'. In her right hand she is holding a red rose, the symbol for England. In style and design the Hever Castle and the National Portrait Gallery portraits are very similar except that in the latter one, Anne's hands are not shown and she looks slightly older as the painter accentuated the dark circles or wrinkles around her eyes. As opposed to photographs, painted portraits will never be able reveal how the portrayed person looked like in reality. People can be painted younger, older or more beautiful as they in fact are or were, see Anne of Cleves. Thus, painted portraits can be, as already mentioned, rather inaccurate, even manipulative. They only give a rough idea of the sitter's physical appearance. As a result, everyone who looks at a painted portrait can create their own image of the person's looks and interpret the portrait in their individual way. And this is something the creators of *The Tudors* certainly did with their character Anne Boleyn. Around the existing portraits of her and the written works describing her physical appearance, *The Tudors* recreated its very own re-imagined Anne Boleyn. Certainly, with regard to the criticism concerning

---

8 See pages 152-153 in Weir for further information on portraits of Anne Boleyn.

accuracy of historical appropriations on screen, painted portraits prove more advantageous as perhaps photographs, as they provide more leeway and freedom in the recreation of a historical person, as the painted images themselves can be inaccurate and the image of the person's appearance is not as fixed as in a photograph.

The choice who would portray Anne Boleyn in *The Tudors* fell on the English actress Natalie Dormer. Before Dormer had been cast as Henry's second wife, she was a relatively unknown actress. She had a minor part in Lasse Halström's 2005 period epic *Casanova* as one of the eponymous hero's love interests Victoria, where she was able to gain first experiences in wearing pompous historical dresses. In an article Dormer explains: "[...] my first day onset (in Venice) was so hot, I was straddling a fan with five layers of petticoats around my waist." In *The Tudors* she again had to do without comfortable twenty-first century costumes remarking "I'm tainted by the corset – Helena Bonham Carteritis" (Armstrong). So one could presume that the casting directors of *The Tudors* were precisely looking for an actress like Dormer to play Anne Boleyn who had already appeared on the screen in an historical costume, which again, far-fetched it may be, allows for a certain intertexuality, as it is for instance they case with named actress Helena Bonham Carter, who is famous for regularly appearing in great costume dramas.

There is another interesting detail concerning Natalie Dormer being cast as Anne Boleyn. Astonishingly, the English actress is a descendant of Jane Dormer, a lady-in-waiting to Anne Boleyn's step-daughter Mary I., the daughter of Henry VIII. and his first wife Katherine of Aragon (Eden). So in choosing Dormer to portray Anne Boleyn, amazingly, the producers of the show were able to establish a bloodline-like link from *The Tudors'* set to the real Tudor court of the sixteenth century. Whether this is a coincidence stands to question.

Yet, is that link sufficient to portray a credible Anne Boleyn? When history is put on screen one of the first things that people will take notice of is how their own already established image, transported via portraits, paintings, photographs or even a video recording (for modern history) of the historical figure in question is played out, so plainly speaking their physical appearance. It is expected, even required, that the film makers choose actors that bear as many similarities in looks as possible with the historical figure. Thus, it was no surprise with how much criticism *The Tudors* had to deal for casting Rhys Meyers as Henry VIII. When looking back at images 01 and 03 it becomes immediately clear that the actor does not look the least like Henry VIII. Screenwriter Hirst has defended his choice of actor as follows: "I pitched Henry as a young, glamorous, athletic, sexy...etc., king because I was fed up with his English iconic version as a fat, bearded monster with a vast ego and even vaster sexual appetite, and very little brain" (*Good to Be King* xii). Executive producer Morgan O'Sullivan adds that "we still want him to be appealing. We don't want to destroy his good looks. An exact portrayal of Henry is not a factor that we think is important" (Irvine). Regardless of whether this is an apt justification, the result is that the Henry VIII. reimagined in *The Tudors* (at least from season one to three, as the producers let him age visibly for the final season) is a young, virile and attractive man, which, at any event, corresponds to descriptions of the young Henry by his contemporaries, as for instance by the Venetian ambassador Giustinian who claimed that, "His Majesty is the handsomest potentate I ever set eyes on [...] Nature could not have done more for him. He is very fair, his whole frame admirably proportioned" (Weir 72). It is often forgotten that the King only turned into the "fat, bearded" Holbein Henry when he was getting older. It was only after 1533 that he started to gain weight, to lose his hair and became less active (Weir 290). But as a young man he was supposedly as much desirable as actor Rhys Meyers. Nevertheless, even as a young Henry, Rhys Meyers does not very much resemble Henry in colouring and size. He is not very tall and instead of Henry's characteristic red hair, Rhys Meyers has brown hair, which is again proof of *The Tudors*' new point of departure and innovative retracing procedure. What is worth mentioning in the context of Rhys Meyer's Henry is the portrayal of the Duke of Buckingham (Steven Weddington) in the series. Being of Plantagenet blood, he considers himself to be to the true heir to the throne. He plots against Henry to overthrow him and is therefore executed in the second episode of season one. The Duke of Buckingham is tall, has red hair and a beard and thus bears more similarity to the historical Henry than Rhys Meyers does. But it can be suggested that his execution is symbolical for the dismissal of the traditional representation of Henry in the programme. Hirst's Henry conveys a totally new interpretation of the English monarch. Henry VII.I has never been illustrated in this modality (*Good to Be King* xiv). And this argument is also applicable to Dormer's Anne Boleyn, as will be subsequently demonstrated.

The first time Anne Boleyn is seen in *The Tudors* is in one of the last scenes of the very first episode of season one.[9] A caption informs the viewers that for this scene the previously shown royal palaces in England are abandoned and that they new setting is now Paris, France. Thomas Boleyn (Nick Dunning), in a previous scene with King Henry, has been entrusted to function as an ambassador for the upcoming summit between King

---

9 Referenced episodes of *The Tudors* are taken from the DVD set *The Tudors: Seasons 1&2*, by Michael Hirst, DVD, Sony Pictures Home Entertainment, 2008. The episodes will be referenced as follows: for example *Tud.* 2.3.10-12 refers to a scene running from minute ten to twelve (for matters of simplicity the minute readings are rounded) from season two, episode three.

Francis and King Henry, the Field of Cloth of Gold. As the summit takes place on French territory, he is sent back to his lodgings in Paris where he is already awaited by his daughters Anne and Mary. The two of them impatiently look out of the window in anticipation of their father's return which brings to mind "Daddy is home!" scenes from modern-day television shows as for example *Desperate Housewives*. Thomas Boleyn tells his daughters about the summit and that they will have the chance to meet the King of England. Both sisters appear rather girlish, young and innocent but in contrast to a dully laughing Mary, Anne already has a dignified, mysterious air around her. Their father toasts them to their futures and an upper body close-up of Anne is shown. She is smiling engagingly which directly hints to the effect the real Anne Boleyn must have had on people. Also, in her physical appearance Dormer bears a number of similarities with Anne Boleyn, which might be necessary for a credible illustration. To begin with, the first glimpse that the observer catches of Anne is her very long dark brown hair when she is staring out of the window, her back turned to the camera. Also, in the later upper body close-up it can be seen that some features of Dormer's face resemble those of the Anne Boleyn shown in the portraits, as for instance Dormer's high cheekbones, her pointy chin and her small mouth. She even has some light moles on her cheeks. But instead of Anne's long and thin face, Dormer has a heart-shaped face with light-blue eyes instead of Anne's black eyes that she had been praised for by her contemporaries. Nevertheless, no matter if black or blue, Dormer's light-blue eyes have an intense gaze that immediately captivates the audience, thus alluding to the same effect as Anne's black eyes had on the Tudor courtiers. Although beauty is mostly in the eye of the beholder, actress Natalie Dormer certainly is everything that is considered beautiful by contemporary standards and thus is not, in contrast to Anne Boleyn, a woman one would think as unconventionally pretty. In the press, Dormer is described as a "traffic-stopping brunette with diamond-slicing cheekbones" who has charmed the critics with her "blend of innocence and sensuality" (Armstrong). Surprisingly, Dormer does not consider herself as a standardized beauty. In an article she says that "people do say that I have a mischievous face" and that she knows "that I'm not a conventional beauty. You can read a lot of painful things on the internet, which criticise you aesthetically" (Paton). But conventionally beautiful or not, undeniably, Dormer has a face that attracts attention - in a positive sense. Like Anne Boleyn, she looks very exotic and extraordinary which the producers also attempted to emphasize by displaying her in contrast to her sister Mary who was considered the more attractive by Early Modern standards. In the previously described scene, the contrast of the two sisters is not that great at first sight, as they wear very similar, unremarkable dresses. But another

23

scene shows Mary and Anne Boleyn at the Field of Cloth of Gold and here Anne clearly makes a case in point that she had something that made her stand out from other women (*Tud.* 1.2.12). In this scene, King Francis brags about regularly "riding his English mare," that is Mary Boleyn, with the result that Henry takes notice of her and asks her to her chambers, which Mary proudly tells her sister Anne. The look Anne gives Mary reveals that she is somehow happy for her sister but also jealous for her being favoured by the King. Mary Boleyn is portrayed as a pretty but naïve, almost dumb girl. She is constantly giggling and the fact that she has already been Francis' mistress and will now also be Henry's shows that she is presented as a girl of loose morals. Mary is beautiful in a conventional sense but next to a mysteriously glancing Anne Boleyn, she seems rather boring and plain, which is also accentuated in their respective clothing. Anne wears a dark crimson dress, which contributes to her sinister mysteriousness, in contrast to Mary who wears a lighter purple and pink dress. If *The Tudors* were a modern American high school series, Mary would be the popular but dull cheerleader that falls for the handsome football player, and Anne would be the mysterious and aloof outsider who is the actual heroine of the story, as for example in *Buffy the Vampire Slayer.*[10] Buffy Summers (Sarah Michelle Gellar) presents that underdog central character whereas she is standing in contrast to the high school's most popular girl and cheerleader Cordelia Chase played by Charisma Carpenter (Elias). Again this example, digressive as it might perhaps seem, works to highlight an element of contemporariness in the portrayal of Anne Boleyn in *The Tudors* as, in this context, her character is illustrated in a similar modus operandi as that of other popular American television shows set in the present.

As the previously analysed promotional shots of Anne and Henry have already validated, "*The Tudors*' Anne Boleyn doesn't exactly match the dowdy creature described by some historical sources," as Deacon claims in an newspaper article. And even though the historical Anne Boleyn could not exactly have been "dowdy," she certainly could not have been as beautiful as Natalie Dormer. Dormer surely has the same exoticness and mysteriousness about her as the real Anne must have had, but that is not sufficient for an USA targeted show. Additionally, the Anne Boleyn of the television programme had to be reinvented more attractively and desirably as her historical counterpart: "It [*The Tudors*] was made for America, so there's going to be a certain aesthetic" (Deacon). The audience wants people they can admire and look up to and this is often, superficially, achieved via physical attractiveness. As a result, Dormer's Anne Boleyn is very much adapted to twenty-

---

10 An American television show created by Joss Whedon that ran from 1997 to 2003, see IMDb.

first century standards of beauty. This is furthermore due to the fact that the audience needed to comprehend Henry's obsession for her. Therefore, the audience had to be as ensnared by her attractiveness and person as Henry is in the show, a little like "Who would not dismiss the Pope for a beauty like Anne Boleyn?."

The "beautiful portrayal" is furthermore achieved through omission of Anne Boleyn's ageing process throughout the years depicted in *The Tudors* as ageing in general is a less marketable factor in mainstream American television, especially for women. The first time Anne is shown is presumably a couple of weeks before the Field of Cloth of Gold took place, so in early 1520. Her portrayal in *The Tudors* then obviously ends with her execution on May 19, 1536. Hence, the audience takes part in sixteen years of Anne's life during which she unnaturally does not age the slightest. There are two possible years of birth of Anne Boleyn and until now historians are not yet certain which year the correct one is. Until recently, it had been believed that Anne was born sometime in 1507, but a more realistic estimation places her date of birth at around 1501-1502.[11] It can be argued that the producers of the show apparently agreed with the latter date as Anne would then have been around 18-19 years old during the Field of Cloth of Gold as opposed to thirteen years old for which a young teenage actor would have been necessary to be cast as Anne Boleyn. During the filming of the first season, actress Natalie Dormer, born in 1982, must have been between twenty-four and twenty-five, so still half a decade older than Anne was during the French and English summit. In contemporary American television programmes and films it is common to have teenage characters be played by actors/actress in their early to mid-twenties because supposedly that is when a human being, especially a female one, is at their peak of beauty. This for examples applies again for Sarah Michelle Gellar who was twenty when she was cast as sixteen-year-old Buffy Summers (Elias) or Rachel Bilson portraying teenager Summer Roberts in the high school drama *The O.C.* (2003-2007) when she had already been twenty two years old (O'Toole). Nevertheless, Dormer has a very innocent, young even "baby-faced" look about her (Paton) which she does not forfeit as she turns older in the course of the series. This then certainly works against a credible depiction of Anne Boleyn in her later years since it has been recorded that she aged prematurely due to the turbulences of the time after the king had fallen in love with her, including the seven-year struggle for an annulment of Henry's marriage to Katherine of Aragon and the related fact that she thus had to keep Henry at a physical distance to remain a virgin, their first child being a daughter and not the long desired and needed male

---

11 For further information on the issue of Anne Boleyn's date of birth see Weir 146-147.

heir to the English throne, her failed pregnancies, Henry's waxing interest in other women including Jane Seymour and last but not least her trial and condemnation. In 1536, the Spanish ambassador Chapuys referred to her as "that thin old woman" which implies that the stress had not only aged her tremendously but had also emaciated her. Anne was no longer the vivacious and youthful female courtier that she was when she came to the Tudor court in between 1524-1525 (Weir 147-59). Nevertheless, *The Tudors* does not realize that fact medially even though that would have been possible within the means and medium of twenty-first century film-making. Make-up, costume and even digital modification are able to let a character age on screen. And that the producers were aware of how to achieve an effect like this is made clear in the last season of the show where Henry and his long-term friend Charles Brandon (Henry Cavil), who has also been in the show ever since the very first episode, eventually are made older with the help of make-up, costume as well as their acting performances.

As it is often the case with historical narratives on screen, it can be difficult for the audience to comprehend that the events depicted in the programme naturally took time to take their course. But due to the given temporal limitations for cinematic history, the viewer may sometimes be under the impression that history happened rapidly. Also in *The Tudors*, every episode is charged with important plot points comprising historical events which in originally took years to unfold. Generally, history on screen has to be made compact. So the duration of the seven long years that Anne had to wait until she could be Henry's wife is difficult for the viewer to comprehend as this is reduced on screen to a time span of only about seven hours. Having Anne's character naturally age during that time would thus have made it easier for the audience to understand the concept of time in *The Tudors*. But of course a contemporary Anne Boleyn on American television cannot be subject to the law of nature. She remains young, beautiful and attractive throughout the years. As with Rhys Meyers as Henry VIII., the show's producers were not willing to turn Dormer into the unattractive "thin old woman" Anne Boleyn became in her later years.

To consolidate this argument, it needs to be mentioned that there are only few moments when *The Tudors*' Anne Boleyn is not perfectly made up. For instance, when Anne falls ill with the sweating sickness in 1528, she is presented lying in bed only wearing a simple white nightgown as opposed to the magnificent dresses she is normally wearing. Her long brown hair hangs loosely and uncombed around her shoulders, this time not accentuated with pearls or bejewelled head pieces. Her face is pale, sweaty and without any traces of make-up (*Tud.* 1.8.46). This also goes for the scene when Anne gives birth to Elizabeth (*Tud.* 2.3.45). If one assumes that Anne's year of birth is the earlier one of 1502,

Anne would already have been thirty-one years old then. But regardless of her age and the exhaustion of childbirth, Anne Boleyn is illustrated comely and maidenly. Even in the execution scene (*Tud.* 2.10.37) of the final episode of season two, Anne, who should be at an age of thirty-seven by then, appears to be as beautiful, youthful and healthy as in her previously mentioned very first scene. Apart from her eyes which are red and puffy from crying, she is not represented "exhausted and dazed [...] partly the result of two sleepless nights and partly from apprehension" (Weir 335) as the real Anne Boleyn appeared on the scaffold on her final day on Earth, according to historical sources.

The portrayal of Anne Boleyn as a young and beautiful woman also functions to establish a contrast to Henry VIII.'s first wife Katherine of Aragon. Even though not unattractive, unlike Dormer Maria Doyle Kennedy cannot be compared to a model from the cover of a fashion magazine. Furthermore, she is almost two decades older than Dormer. The producers surely put a lot of emphasis on the age factor where the love triangle between Katherine, Henry and Anne is concerned. The historical Katherine of Aragon was merely six years older than Henry, yet in *The Tudors* she is re-imagined almost fifteen years older than the young and vibrant Henry. Intentionally, their difference in age is portrayed more drastically than it actually was, which of course makes it comprehensible, even more logical, that Henry pursues the young Anne Boleyn. As a result, visually the couple Henry and Katherine do not harmonise that greatly. In her behaviour as well as clothing Katherine appears rather pious and reasonable as opposed to the king who is presented like a modern day rock star, or as *Time* writes, "a kind of Tudor Mick Jagger in his prime." So certainly the audience can justify Henry's pursuit of the young and sensuous Anne Boleyn, who, both visually and in spirit, has more in common with him than Katherine. This contrast is furthermore perceptible by their respective costumes, a point that will be picked up in the thesis' chapter on Anne Boleyn's costumes.

Overall, by her sheer looks, *The Tudors* portrays Anne Boleyn according to what is typical for mainstream American television shows, that is as a woman of admirable beauty. Thus, the desirable young actress Natalie Dormer, who could also be successful as a photo model, as images 01 and 03 have proven, was cast as Anne Boleyn. The character's appearance was very loosely built around the existing portraits of its historical counterpart whereas the producers, by casting Dormer, were successful in making Dormer's Anne Boleyn evoking the similar mesmerizing effect the actual wife of Henry VIII. had had on her contemporaries.

3. Art Thou Not a Virtuous Maid? - Portraying Anne's Personality and Behaviour in *The Tudors*

The previous chapter has attempted to demonstrate to what extent Anne Boleyn of *The Tudors* seems contemporized merely by her visual nature. But how is this contemporariness realized in the representation of her behaviour and conduct throughout the twenty episodes she plays a main part? Both this aspect and the transformation that Anne's character will be subject to within her portrayal will be considered in this part of the thesis.

Clearly, the role of women in the sixteenth century and the role of women today in our western world is entirely different. Generally speaking, two movements were responsible for a transformation of the female image in the sixteenth century. These are humanism and Protestantism which both started in the early sixteenth century. Protestantism advocated spiritual equality, thus making it possible for women to read, interpret, debate and even preach the Scriptures. Humanism attempted an elevation of woman and a retrieval from her low status which had been assigned to her by medieval Christian doctrine. The concept of marriage also underwent a redefinition as an institution not only for sinless procreation but also for mutual comfort and companionship. Generally, women's passive qualities were praised such as sexual purity. This required female chastity stood in direct connection with a woman's speech, silence being considered another principal virtue of woman. Women were also primarily defined by their functions as mothers and wives, not as an individual that had her own desires and needs. Furthermore, it was forbidden for women to express their opinion in public and to partake male activities. Early humanists argued favourably for women's education but nevertheless the overall objective of instructing woman was to turn them into virtuous and wise wives (Krontiris 3-12).

But for women at court slightly more liberal definitions of female behaviour applied. This was mainly due to courtesy books, principles of ideal conduct at court, like Baldassare Castiglione's *The Book of the Courtier* published in 1528.[12] These books emphasized the new 'polite' society which demanded more from women as merely the skill of reading and writing, but also encouraged them to partake activities assigned to men. In contrast to the female virtue of silence for ordinary women, ladies at court were advised to take part in conversations with controlled speech and gesture. Instead of holding her tongue, a woman of the Early Modern court should be able to manipulate speech

---

12 For further information see Baldassare Castiglione, *The Book of the Courtier*, trans. George Bull (Harmondswoth: Penguin Books, 1986).

effectively. It was expected of women to take part in polite conversation with male courtiers, thus remaining silent was no longer considered virtuous. Of course, speech of the ladies at court was still connected to sexuality. In that context, Castiglione cautions about the several traps a court lady has to avoid in order to maintain a chaste image, as a reputation for sexual availability would minimize any prospects for a successful marriage. Certainly the demands for female speech are contradictory to those of female chastity, but it is required of a court lady to balance them skilfully. She is supposed to evaluate what male courtiers might say or do and has to prevent them from responding in a manner that could be disadvantageous for her. Furthermore, a court lady is advised to not only take an defensive stance but also to put herself skilfully on display. This has of course to be realized without obviously wanting to attract attention. Using gestures for emphasis was desired but the first and foremost skill was effective speech (Krontiris 14-15).

Hence, as opposed to life for ordinary women, life for women at court, concerning definitions of gender, was, for sixteenth century standards rather advanced and modern. But how modernized is female behaviour depicted in *The Tudors*? How much has *The Tudors'* Anne Boleyn been influenced by twenty-first century definitions of femininity? To begin with, it is essential to explore what kind of woman the historical Anne Boleyn was, in order to contrast her to her portrayal in the television programme. When Anne came to the English court, she appeared to embody everything that was expected of a respectable lady at court. With her outstanding social skills, she was able to draw the admiration of many courtiers to her, as well as that of the King's. She was highly sophisticated, witty and intelligent, sweet and joyous. According to the courtly ideal female, she took great pleasure in participating in male activities such as hunting, playing bowls or gambling since she knew how to play cards and dice. Anne Boleyn liked tasting wine and took pleasure in a joke. Also her artistic skills were beyond comparison. She was a very talented singer, musician and dancer (Weir 153-54). Thus, her conversational and behavioural skills were according to how Castiglione described them for the ideal lady at court. She managed to be both chaste and flirtatious in the game of courtly love, always finding the balance between being charming and engaging, and between being discreet and modest. Furthermore, her continental training, as she had served at the court of Margaret of Austria and had been a lady-in-waiting to the French Queen Claude, added to the fascination she evoked in the English courtiers. In England she seemed unique, exuding the elegance of the French court the English courtiers attempted to counterfeit. Anne's excellent behaviour and gesture exceeded that of all the other ladies at court according to Wolsey trying to justify Henry's obsession for Anne (Lindsey 50-55).

Anne's artistic skills are for example used in *The Tudors* for the scene when Henry first sets his eyes on her (*Tud.* 1.3.8-12). As Henry is already tiring of his mistress Mary Boleyn, Thomas Boleyn and the Duke of Norfolk (Anne's uncle) are planning to trade in Anne for her sister and put her before the King's eyes in order that the Boleyn family remains favoured by him. Hence, Thomas Boleyn bribes a courtier to secure Anne a place as one of the performers in a masked pageant for the Spanish envoys. In the pageant the 'graces' such as Kindness, Honour, Mercy and Pity, which are played by the ladies, are kept in a papier mâché castle and are then rescued by the male courtiers representing Youth, Devotion, Pleasure, Loyalty etc. The also masked King is amongst them portraying Honesty. Unaware that she is ironically predicting her fate, Anne was given the role of Perseverance in the performance, as is really known from the historical record. In an extremely Hollywoodized scene, Honesty of course climbs up to Perseverance where they stare intensely at each other for the first time. He then takes her hand and tells her that she now is is prisoner. She lets go of his hand and runs away. This scene is quite resemblant of the scene of Baz Luhrmann's very modern adaptation of Shakespeare's *Romeo and Juliet* of 1997 when Romeo (Leonardo DiCaprio) and Juliet (Claire Danes) lock eyes for the first time behind an aquarium (25-29). Although they do not meet at a masked pageant for the first time, they meet at a masked ball. The similarity in dress of the two respective couples is remarkable. Both Juliet and Anne are wearing white, angel-like dresses and their male counterparts are both dressed up as knights. Juliet runs away from that first encounter as her nurse approaches her, so does Anne Boleyn. Both these escapes from the two knights are followed by a dance, whereas Juliet has to dance with Count Paris and Anne with Charles Brandon, who is then finally displaced by Henry. The similarities in these two scenes are striking. What is noticeable is that this cinematic adaptation of *Romeo and Juliet* is a much contemporized version of Shakespeare's tragedy with the exception the Shakespearean language is still kept. Set in an imagined twentieth century Verona, daggers are replaced by guns, Romeo takes drugs and Mercutio dresses up as a drag-queen dancing to disco music. So it can be argued that the parallels of these scenes hint at the contemporariness in the portrayal of Renaissance matter, thus establishing an intertextual connection.

This episode and the previous, episode two, of *The Tudors* also depict quite realistically, how women were supposedly used as instruments by their male relatives for securing a family's good fortunes. At the end of episode two of the first season, the viewer sees how Anne, not knowing the reason for it, is summoned by her father and uncle from Paris to England (*Tud.* 1.2.47-50). Obediently, she kneels down before the men of her family who glance at each other mischievously, like two predators ready to attack their prey. Norfolk then leaves. The focus is now on Anne and her father who is playing with a falcon while he explains his daughter what he has planned for her. He tells her that the King is already tiring of her sister Mary, thus the family's fortunes and influence are falling. He discloses to her that he now expects her to become the King's mistress. A close-up of her face reveals that she is not pleased with her father's plan. Yet, she responds in an obedient way, as expected of her, but at the same time she tries to get herself out of her father's scheming asking: "Even if he had me. Who is to say he would keep me?". She then is advised to play Henry's passions. While he patronisingly strokes her chin in an close-up, Thomas Boleyn tells his daughter: "There's something deep and dangerous in you, Anne. Those eyes of yours are like dark hooks for the soul." Although not dark in colour, the close-up of Anne's face underlines this statement. Anne does not seem content that she is being used as her father's and uncle's puppet, yet she has no other choice than to obey. This is furthermore made clear by the scene's usage of the symbolism of the falcon. At first sight it may only seem that here a typical hobby of a Renaissance noble man is being depicted. But the falcon serves two other functions. The first and the obvious one is that the falcon belongs to Anne Boleyn's badge showing a crowned white falcon who is holding a sceptre, standing on a burning tree stump from which a couple of red and white roses grow. Anne did not choose this to be her badge until she became Queen of England.[13] So using the falcon in this scene suggests a foreshadowing of how her father's plans, which he announces while holding the bird of prey, are going to play out in the future. Furthermore, the falcon itself is symbolic of Anne. When the scene starts, the camera has its focus on the falcon and its light-brown, greenish eyes. Then Anne is seen approaching in the background. The focus then shifts to Anne, blurring the falcon and showing her almost having the same intense expression in her eyes as the falcon. As a bird of prey, a falcon is as "dark and dangerous" as Thomas Boleyn claims his daughter to be. In heraldry the falcon means "one who does not rest until the objective achieved," so it is symbolic of someone who is eagerly pursuing a desired objective. Boleyn has an ambitious objective and Anne resembles the falcon who will obtain it for him (Hidden Meanings, *Tudors Wiki*). Like the falcon, Anne is not a free but a tamed creature, constrained by her father. Both the falcon's and Anne's wild nature are subdued by him: the first because it is an animal, the latter because she is a female. A woman was not free to make her own decision as she was ruled by her father or other male family members

---

13 On Anne Boleyn's badge, read Eric Ives, *The Life and Death of Anne Boleyn* (Oxford et al.: Blackwell, 2004) 220-222.

and later by her husband. This scene of *The Tudors* authentically portrays that Anne had no other choice than to obey to her father's wishes as her sister Mary had already done before. No contemporary post-feminist spirit can be respected in the realization of that scene since, if Anne had rebelled against her inflicted ordeal, she would have refused to do as her father and uncle pleased and never tried to gain Henry's affection. Surely, her course of life would have been different.

In the beginning of episode three of season one, it is once more shown how Anne is used by her uncle and father to fulfil their interests and ambitions. Anne is not present in the scene while Norfolk and Boleyn discuss her future. Norfolk says: "Once she opens her legs for him, she can open her mouth and denounce Wolsey" (*Tud.* 1.3.8). Against the Early Modern female virtue of chastity, the two men are willing to use Anne's sexuality for political reasons. Her absence in this decision made over her head (literally) shows that her opinion is of no importance.

In contrast to the later denouncements of Anne as "the King's whore", *The Tudors* (initially) takes the stance that Anne Boleyn was indeed a chaste, virtuous woman. In one scene she can be seen lying on a meadow under a tree at the Boleyn family home at Hever Castle together with her admirer the poet Thomas Wyatt. He reads a poem to her and then tries to kiss her. She commands him to stop as he is already a married man (*Tud.* 1.3.20-24). Lindsey writes that the historical Anne was presumably attracted to the handsome poet but was too afraid to risk any prospects of a successful marriage having an affair with a man who is already married. Instead she chose the safer path of playing the courtly role of the unreachable beloved (56), something that has been realized in the show.

But even though *The Tudors* aims to portray an honourable Anne Boleyn, the makers also, at the same time, want to use her or the actress's sex appeal for reasons of marketability. Thus, a dream sequence of Henry fantasizing about his new object of affection is integrated into the previously mentioned episode (*Tud.* 1.3.42-45). Here, Henry chases Anne along the halls of an empty Whitehall Palace. Once he has caught her, she tells him: "No. Not like this." He asks then how and she advises him: "Seduce me. Write letters to me. And poems. I love poems. Ravish me with your words. Seduce me." Again, she runs away from him, disappearing behind a door. Henry opens it and sees a naked Anne trying to cover her nude body with her hands intensely staring at him, repeating with this pose her wish to be seduced by him. Henry then wakes up from this dream, covered in sweat.

It seems unlikely that the Anne Boleyn *The Tudors* seeks to portray, namely a

33

perfectly virtuous female of the Tudor court, would have permitted herself to let all her clothes fall to the floor in order to attract Henry's attention. But still, it had been necessary to emphasize her desirability for both Henry and the audience, simultaneously not letting her appear as a woman of loose morals. Hence, applying a dream sequence was a smart way of reconciling these two opposing stances. The dream sequence also functions to demonstrate how besotted Henry eventually became with Anne Boleyn and allows the spectator to plunge into Henry's world of thought, similar to a stream of consciousness. Furthermore, the dream symbolizes the point of origin for Henry's courtship of Anne. In the previous two episodes, the audience has seen the King taking Bessie Blount and then Mary Boleyn as his mistresses. In the show, these two women are depicted as wantons to be easily seduced and conquered. Anne had to be illustrated differently. She asks for the full programme of courtship (poems, letters) which Henry is most willingly to give her. This is a recurring theme in contemporary romantic films. The girl who distinguishes herself from the other girls, who plays or is in fact hard to get and does not let herself be conquered that easily, is the one who in the end gets the "prince". A very successful adaptation of Shakespeare's *The Taming of the Shrew* picks up this vintage theme again. In the high-school film *10 Things I Hate About You* (directed by Gil Junger, 1999) Katarina Stratford (Julia Stiles), a non-conformist feminist, does not participate in the on-going dating culture of her peers. She is even appalled by it. But in the end, although or probably because she is different from all the other girls of her high-school, she finds the love of her life (Holden). Fortunately, the film (or play) is a comedy, so she is spared the tragic ending, unlike Anne

Anne's morality is once more put into focus in a scene when Henry, already madly in love with her, comes to visit her at Hever Castle (*Tud.* 1.5.10-13). He offers her to become his official mistress and promises that he will serve exclusively her. Anne is very upset about this offer and asks the King: "What have I done to make you treat me like this?" Henry is confused about her response. She explains to him: "I have already given my maidenhead into my husband's hands. And whoever he is, only he will have it. [...] Because I know how it goes otherwise. My sister is called "the great prostitute" by everyone." Here it is shown how fast a woman, in this case Anne's sister, is cast into disreputability by light behaviour. Anne refuses to meet the same fate. Even though the audience knows from a previous episode that Anne is advised by her father and uncle to play the King's passions, it is convincingly depicted that she honestly means what she says about her maidenhead, and her troubled facial expression lets the spectator guess that she also has sincere feelings for Henry but is uncertain to deal with them.

In another scene of the same episode, Henry again consumed by his desire for Anne, tries to claim her maidenhead (*Tud.* 1.3.36-39). They are both passionately kissing in a bedchamber in Hever Castle. They are both drunk with love but Anne is persistent, even though it becomes evident that this is very hard for as she also has physical needs. But Henry is able to control himself telling her: "I shall honour your maidenhead until we are married. No less can I do for love:" Anne seems genuinely content with Henry's declaration of love and respect assuring him: "Oh, love. And by daily proof you shall me find, to be to you both loving and kind."

Although this scene is very physical with Henry eagerly caressing Anne's body and kissing her breasts and thus serving to contribute to reviews about *The Tudors* showing "history as sexed-up, simplified storylines" (Sessions), the characters' respective effort to remain chaste and respectful of a future, much hoped for marriage in spite of their sexual yearning for each other also endows the characters with personality. Wray notices that it is typical of contemporary American television dramas to emphasize personality over narrative, which functions to encourage identification through bustling, yet at the same time intimate camera work. Not only strives the show to get to the bottom of Henry's internal life, but also that of the other characters, whose interior ambitions, objectives and attitudes are introduced and elaborated across the years (40-41). In the same manner, Dormer's Anne Boleyn is created. Her story is told but always with a special stress on her personality with the aim to make her more accessible to the general audience. She show manages not to merely narrate that Anne had a relationship with Henry, but also how and into which direction this relationship developed. Anne for example confesses to her family that in the beginning she did not like it so much to win Henry's affection, that she did not care for the King but now this has changed. Norfolk then reminds her not to be "fooled by your own masquerade" and that "it is your duty to use the King's love to our advantage in supplanting Wolsey." But Anne's facial expression reveals that it is against her will to use Henry's infatuation for her family's scheming and that she herself is being used as a tool for that end (*Tud.* 1.6.2-5). Coincidentally, Wolsey calls Anne a silly girl about which she is rather angered. As a result, feeling unjustly treated by the cardinal, she now has her own motives for destroying Wolsey's power and influence, which only coincides with those of Thomas Boleyn and Norfolk. This is supposed to demonstrate that Anne has a mind of her own and that she realizes as the King's affection for her is growing she is beginning to wield more power than her patronising male relatives and that she eventually can use her clever mind to her own advantage. For Anne this certainly is a novelty regarding the gender-based restrictions she had been previously exposed to. Throughout twenty episodes it is depicted how Anne develops from a young girl being used as a tool by her father and uncle into a strong, ambitious woman, who benefits from her waxing influence to forward her own causes, also in religious matters. The historical Anne Boleyn was considered to have been a rather outspoken woman, which often went beyond the courtly ideal of female conversational skills. But which also shows that she was and is also portrayed as a woman who was well ahead of her time. In that *The Tudors* depicts Anne Boleyn favourably, someone who the general audience finds themselves sympathizing with. There are several historians that take a very hostile position towards Anne Boleyn, claiming that she had no feelings for Henry and that she was only driven by raw ambition to become the next Queen of England, at any cost (Lindsey 59-60). Hirst has aimed for an entirely different interpretation of Anne Boleyn. He intended to portray her in a way that people could feel for her and try to understand in what difficult situation she was in. In contrast to her, partly still continuing, unpopularity, Hirst attempts to show what a burden Anne had to carry having the love of a king, being forced into this by her male family members, and willingly destroying a marriage (Season 2 Podcast). The writer also believes that the love between Anne and Henry was true and that he highly valued Anne's outspokenness and intelligence. In a scene, when we see her for the first time meddling with Henry's affairs concerning Wolsey, she realizes that she "spoke of things I should not." But Henry assures her: "I give you leave that we may always speak freely with each other. Honestly, openly and with a true heart. For me, that is the true definition of love (*Tud.* 1.6.6-8)." It can be argued that the makers of the show included that scene to justify Anne's later involvement in religious and political affairs as well as the fact that she is never afraid to speak her mind. Henry encourages her to do so, thus it seems perfectly justified for her and the audience and not the least unusual. After all, she only obeys her husband. That Henry is, however, unable to keep that promise in the later years seemingly is not Anne's fault.

It is necessary to mention that even though the show portrays Anne Boleyn in a positive light, it does not automatically portray Queen Katherine in a negative one. In the end, the audience feels for both women (or even for his entire six wives) regardless of whether they are competing for Henry's love. *The Tudors* successfully manages to depict all of their characters' motives in a way that the observer can comprehend their actions, even if these motives seem less honourable. In a later scene of the previously mentioned episode, Anne fulfilling her duties as Katherine's lady-in-waiting is shown washing Queen Katherine's feet, kneeling before her. This clearly is a very demeaning posture for Anne but as she is demeaned physically, so is Katherine mentally, knowing of her husband's

36

relationship to her young and beautiful lady-in-waiting. While Anne is washing Katherine's feet, the Queen notices that Anne is wearing an expensive necklace, evidently a gift from the King. Katherine, thereupon, designates her as an expensive whore. Anne seems extremely hurt by the Queen's insult, objecting in a humble, almost child-like voice: "I am no whore, your Majesty. I love His Majesty. I believe he loves me." Katherine answers: "He is infatuated by you, as men often are by new things. Soon he will see for what you really are. And he will tire of you, as all the others" (*Tud.* 1.6.36-38). The audience feels both for Katherine, who is about to be disposed by a younger woman, and also for Anne who only wants to become the wife of the man she genuinely loves. Although Katherine treats Anne despitefully, as she calls her a whore, one can understand her action. Any woman would feel equally if her husband had traded her for a younger model, no matter if this concerns a sixteenth century queen or a twenty-first century housewife. And this is exactly the reason why *The Tudors* has such an appeal to a contemporary audience. While narrating events which happened almost five-hundred years ago, it attaches importance on occurrences that will never be outdated, thus building a bridge to the present.

Hirst states that the main audience of *The Tudors* are women (interviewed by Gomeshi). This can be explained by the series' general modus operandi of introducing and expanding female characters. Particularly Henry's wives are imported and given major roles (Wray 33, 42). So of course the love-triangle between Katherine, Henry and Anne is an attractive issue to be portrayed, whereas the show seeks to emphasize the difference of the two competing women. Hirst has the opinion that Doyle Kennedy symbolizes birthright and majesty which sits easily on her shoulders, hence her performance of a queen is extremely convincing. The aspect for casting Dormer as Anne Boleyn thus had to be different. For him it was necessary to give the part to an inexperienced actress like Dormer. Dormer was rather nervous to play a part on which a lot of importance weighs, and like Anne Boleyn she had to grow into that part. Both Anne Boleyn and Dormer are learning at the same time (Hirst, Season 2 Podcast). But this is not the only parallel between the actress and the historical figure she is portraying. Like Anne Boleyn, she is a very commanding and enthusiastic person saying that she even sometimes "might seem a bit of a handful to directors because I have been told that I have a very dominant personality" (Paton). Journalist Stephen Armstrong describes Dormer as having a sharp academic mind, being surprised at her level of preparation for his interview with her. Unlike any other young actress, she made herself familiar with some of the writer's articles, quoting his own words back at him. This clearly evokes similarities to Anne Boleyn's sharp wit and intelligence. Also, the actress had to stand her ground in the boy's boarding school (that admits girls in the senior grade) she attended. Like Anne Boleyn she is trained in dancing and enjoys participating in typically male activities, a requirement for the ideal court lady, such as playing poker and fencing (in the London Fencing Academy). Coincidentally, Dormer also has a brother and a sister. Thus, by comparing Dormer to Boleyn, it can be suggested that the producers of the show intentionally cast an actress as Anne Boleyn that shared some main traits of character with the historical counterpart. This again brings together the present and the past which serves the contemporary spirit in *The Tudors*. According to the argument: if Natalie Dormer portrays a very contemporary Anne Boleyn, an Anne Boleyn adapted to the twenty-first century, the actress and the historical figure must share some parallels. Additionally, in an era where people are obsessed with celebrity, the actor and the part they are portraying, often become inseparable. And if the actor/actress and his/her role exhibit a variety of similarities, the boundaries between fiction and reality are even blurring more smoothly, which then gives the audience the impression that within in that fictional character they somehow experience the 'real' person.

* * *

Anne's strong will and ambitiousness is also increasingly used to re-imagine the way she attempted to forward her own causes in religious matters. Anne learns throughout the episodes that the rise of the Luther's teachings might prove convenient for guaranteeing Henry a divorce from Katherine of Aragon. The series not only depicts Henry Tudor's personal life but also political and religious events (as they are mostly closely connected), such as the English Reformation. Their depiction, however, appears to be rather simplified and abstracted. Selling the English Reformation, and other significant historical milestones, suspensefully, certainly is a difficult task to fulfil, given that the show is targeted to a mainstream audience. Hence, initially an interest in the characters has to be established, as Hirst claims (Wray 50). And, as *The Tudors* is characteristic of stressing the importance of women's roles, Anne is portrayed as a key figure of the Reformation. In episode eight of season one, the audience begins to see how Anne Boleyn increasingly deploys her influence over the King, which progressively encourages her to speak her mind, often ending in her losing her temper, as for example when she and Henry are walking hand in hand in the royal gardens together. They appear everything like an harmonious couple. Anne inquires about the trial concerning the annulment of Henry's marriage to Katherine and he assures her that Wolsey has told him that the Pope is going to decide in his favour. Happily, Anne ascertains that they now can start planning the wedding. Henry kisses her in a reconfirming way, but then the atmosphere of the shifts when Henry tells Anne that he has to share Katherine's table and bed for the sake appearances. Anne grows infuriated with this announcement and is not hesitant to demonstrate her displeasure, hinting at Henry that he might be unfaithful to her once he is back in bed with his wife. Hurt by how little trust Anne holds for him, he storms off. So does Anne but into a different direction which works to symbolize the couples' incipient dissension (*Tud.* 1.8.5-8). The content of their argument again seems timeless and could as well have been from a scene set in the 2000s. Every modern woman would be able to identify herself with Anne and act in the same way as Anne does in that scene. Her reaction does not seem the least bit unusual. Yet, it was in sixteenth the century. Anne not only questions male but also royal authority and is not afraid to say so. Increasingly, the temper that her historical counterpart had been renowned for begins to show. In another scene, she argues heavily with Henry because he again has quarrelled with Katherine about the annulment. Angrily she shouts at the King for having wasted her time and youth waiting for a marriage that to all appearances is never to happen. Infuriated she runs off telling Henry that she is going home to Hever Castle. He begs her to stay, but she ignores his request whereupon he, unavailingly, yells after her "I'm the King of England!" (*Tud.* 1.9.16-17). But she disregards his authority and demonstrates that she has a mind of her own. This is a circumstance, the makers of *The Tudors* did not have to invent. Weir writes that "her thwarted ambition and repressed sexuality had turned her into a virago with a sharp tongue," but Henry was too afraid of losing her that he did not complain about her inappropriate behaviour (219).

At any rate, Anne's, for women of the time atypical, assertiveness combined with her power over the King is deployed in the series to make her the perfect target for Thomas Cromwell (James Frain) to advance the Protestant cause. He comes to see Anne and entrusts her with a book entitled *The Obedience of a Christian Man* by William Tyndale. He explains to her that "it contains many good criticism of the papacy and the arrogance and abuses of priests. You will find it most illuminating. But always and ever be cautious as to whom you show this. You must know it might be accounted heresy even to possess it. And Wolsey is still keen enough to prosecute heretics as we are called who embrace the true religion" (*Tud.* 1.8.10-12). It is interesting that Cromwell gives additional information about what exactly defines a heretic, which suggests that the producers considered it necessary to explain the term, which emphasizes the fact that history is simplified for a mainstream non-academic audience, as both Anne Boleyn and Cromwell would have known what 'heretic' meant.

In the previous episodes, the portrayal of Anne Boleyn's religious perspectives had been rather negligent. The rise of Lutheranism as a threat to the official Catholic faith of the country is gradually introduced to the series through very religiously represented characters, as for example Thomas More (Jeremy Northam). But apart from the depiction of the occasional prayer, Anne has been hitherto left out in the religious discourse for the most part. She only becomes involved when her marital fate is depended on it. So it must seem rather surprising for the viewer that Cromwell uses the 'we' form when he speaks about him and Anne as followers of the true religion as no occurrence in particular had until then hinted at her religious views. Gratefully and without hesitation she accepts the book and immediately begins to read it, suggesting to the audience that Anne indeed is an educated and learned Renaissance woman.

It is of course a dexterous manoeuvre of Anne to wait for a perfect moment to enlighten Henry about the book's content. The moment is ripe when the couple goes riding in a valley surrounded by forest. Henry is mad that he, the King of England, is summoned to Rome to answer for himself in the annulment case. He is infuriated that he has to obey to the authority of the Pope although he theoretically has to answer to no authority but God. Cannily, Anne asks permission to speak plainly to emphasize Henry's authority which in that moment he feels questioned. She enlightens him that there are writers that say that the King has absolute power above all, even the Pope. She asks him: "I have a book to show you, with your permission?," whereupon he unhesitatingly demands to see it (*Tud.* 1.9.25-27). This scene reveals both how cleverly Anne walks on dangerous grounds and with how much sensitivity she manages to boost his ego and pride. Again, as typical for contemporary American television shows, the stress is more on personality than on the narrative. Concerning the episode's plot, this scene has no real function. It only depicts what strategy Anne uses to present the book to Henry. So the focus is on her personality, her character traits. History-wise it is not important how Henry got the book but rather that he did at all. This scene also works to underline Anne's representation as one of the key-figures of the Reformation.

The main plot point concerning how Henry is increasingly involved with the new learnings appears in the final episode of the first season when we see Henry reading aloud from Tyndale's book to Anne (*Tud.* 1.10.8-10). He reads out the passage that says that a king is only accountable to God and no one else, remarking that "this is a book for me and all kings." Anne, all the while sitting majestically and confidently looking in her chair, reveals to him that "there are other books like it. Books which detail the abuse of power, privileges, the greed of the clergy in Your Majesty's realm. Books which Wolsey kept

40

deliberately hidden from you." Henry expresses an eager interest to read them. This intellectual exchange illustrates that Anne is almost at the same level of sophistication with Henry, or even higher as it is she who enlightens him about the new theories, no longer being the subordinate female from the earlier episodes. She has managed to turn the 'Defender of the Faith' (the title which Henry is awarded by the Pope in episode four) towards reformist ideas and thus demonstrates that indeed she is not the "silly girl" Wolsey, who meanwhile has fallen into disgrace, claimed her to be. Particularly for the female audience of *The Tudors* this must be satisfying. Against the restrictions of her sex at that time, Anne eventually has the upper hand over a once powerful man. In spite her cunning scheming against Wolsey, Anne is still presented in a favourable light simply because Wolsey is not. The theme that a clever girl outwits an authoritative man certainly finds its advocates in a post-feminist society.

That Anne's intelligence and perseverance eventually are rewarded is a well-known fact. The second season opens with the caption "And so it begins," possibly referring to the tremendous religious and political changes to come. The audience is informed that it is London in the year 1532. The opening minutes firstly show Henry and Anne attending the holy mass, then Katherine is shown praying, subsequently Thomas More is depicted, also praying. These introductory minutes suggest that the second season's will be most notably concerned with religious matters and the beginning of the English Reformation. Henry breaks with the Church of Rome, makes himself the Supreme Head of the Church of England and marries Anne Boleyn. That Anne Boleyn's progressive beliefs had not only been a means to an end to finally become Queen of England is for the first time expressively demonstrated in a scene when she holds an introductory speech to her new servants after her coronation (*Tud.* 2.3.36-38). Again her morality and religious ambitions are made clear. She instructs her ladies-in-waiting as well as her male attendants to honourable, virtuous, discreet and just conduct, forbidding them to quarrel, to swear and to say evil and lewd things or go to brothels. Furthermore, she suggests them: "I will keep here a copy of Tyndale's English Bible. All of you are free to read it and draw spiritual nourishment from it. For the old days are gone. Everything has changed now. Thanks to His Majesty you have all been delivered from the darkness and bondage of papal thraldom, idolatry, and superstition. This is a new beginning. For me. For you. For England." That the Scripture is conveniently disposed in front of the fireplace with flames bursting behind it can be interpreted as a prediction what the religious change heralded by this Bible will bring in the following decades.

As already been argued, Dormer's Anne Boleyn is without doubt portrayed as a reformist heroine in *The Tudors*. At the same time her religiousness is not depicted in the same way Katherine of Aragon's or Thomas More's is. The real Anne Boleyn had been raised in the traditional faith of Catholicism and she observed Catholic practices until she died. And although Anne had always been sincere in her beliefs, throughout her life she never showed her faithfulness to religion in the same extent and manner as Katherine of Aragon did, with the exception of the last week before her execution. Also, Anne Boleyn was not a Lutheran but she, nevertheless, was a fervent advocate for reform within the Church and held an enlightened attitude towards heretical literature which she encouraged Henry to read (as seen in *The Tudors*) although he had banned those writings (Weir 195-96). While the television programme represents Anne as a key-reforming figure, she is nevertheless shown as someone who is not too absorbed by their religious beliefs, supposedly like the real Anne Boleyn. It seems that her interest in heretical literature stems from intellectual motives rather than religious ones, which would make more sense to a modern audience. Her religious ambitions are just sufficient enough to set the ball rolling but not too expanded in order to construct her in a still appealing way to the contemporary viewer. The reason for this is on the one hand founded in the decreasing religiousness in twenty-first century western societies and on the other hand in the post 9/11 debate about religious fanaticism. Wray argues that "in *The Tudors*, early modern fanaticism and twenty-first-century ideological conflicts are brought together" (36), which proves Toplin's argument that in cinematic history issues of the past are re-interpreted in contemporary terms. She then gives the example from the show of the Jesuit (although the order is yet unfounded) who is sent by Rome to assassinate Anne. As in the modern discourse of the suicide bomber, the Jesuit Brereton is told that if he died as the result of the assassination, his family would be taken care of and heaven would welcome him (Wray 37). Within this issue, especially an American audience might have difficulties sympathising with characters whose religious zeal sometimes even goes as far as martyrdom. Thomas More's persistent and stubborn refusal to swear the oath of the Act of Succession which would make him automatically acknowledging Henry's supremacy over the Church of England, which then eventually leads to his execution and martyrdom, appears exaggerated and troubling and hard to comprehend for the modern viewer. Also Katherine's constant demonstrations of religious devotion become rather onerous after a while. Of course it is difficult to bring the great importance of religion of former centuries to screen in an age where individual confessions do no longer play that significant a part in one's life. Regardless, how religiously devoted the real Anne Boleyn was, in *The Tudors* she has a religious view very much adapted to modernity. The same argument goes for

Henry. On the programme he is constructed as having a marginal and conflicting relationship to God, absolutely opposing Henry VIII.'s traditional image as a devout Christian. This again points to a character distinguished by its contemporariness as the defining signifier (Wray 35-36).

Anne Boleyn's importance as reforming character, a champion of progress, is additionally illustrated in the already mentioned assassination plot against her. The Pope's (Peter O'Toole) remark: "Why doesn't just someone get rid of her" (*Tud.* 2.1.11) suggests her threat to the order of things, and that is the reason she needs to be eliminated. A scene shows Ambassador Chapuys talking to an unknown man who is hiding his face behind a cape. This man tells him about his plan to "dispatch the witch to hell" (*Tud.* 2.1.50-51). In the opening scene of the following episode someone yet again unknown puts three cards on the table. It shows a king card with a capital 'H' and two queen cards with capitals 'A' and 'K'. With a knife the person cuts of the head of the 'A' queen (*Tud.* 2.2.1-3). Anne later finds the cards, noticing: "Here is a book of prophecy. This the King, this is the Queen and this is myself with my head cut off" (*Tud.* 2.2.12-14). This historically happened in almost the same way. Someone hostile towards Anne secretly put a cartoon drawing into her chambers. They drawings showed the same illustration as the cards did in the episode (Lindsey 85-86). This is a great example how *The Tudors* interweaves historical details into the plot and creates an own storyline out of it. Later in the episode the unknown man is again shown pointing a gun, from a hidden angle, at Anne who sits alone by the fire. Before the murder can be committed Henry appears at Anne's side leaving the assassination attempt unsuccessful (*Tud.* 2.2.50-52). The identity of the assassin as William Brereton, a historical figure who was executed along with the four other men accused of having committed adultery with Queen Anne but for the show entirely fictionalized, is only revealed in the subsequent episode, in which he again tries to shot Anne Boleyn during her coronation process (*Tud.* 2.3.27-30). He yet once more fails, missing the shot. The attempt goes unnoticed to the royal couple and Brereton is not caught. Both assassination attempts do not appear in the historical records and thus are in all likelihood fictional. In all likelihood because they could have happened going unnoticed or being covered up. The producers of the show intentionally suggest events to emphasize that history is always selective and/or incomplete and within the medium of film these suggestions can be explored. In the case of the two assassination attempts of Anne Boleyn, it can be argued that Hirst included them to represent her as untouchable and invincible, hence investing her with unnatural power, which is always fascinating for an audience. Furthermore, in a symbolical meaning, it suggests that the spirit of progress,

43

manifested in Anne's character, cannot be so easily fought - at least not for the moment.

Anne's involvement in and commitment to the Reformation is one last time strikingly portrayed in a scene a few scenes prior to her arrest. In an extremely stately manner, Anne comes to see Cromwell accusing him of advising the King to sell the dissolved monasteries to his courtiers "even though the bill has not yet reached the statute book." She continues, "Our Reformation was never meant to be about personal gain. Religious houses should not be sold off, but converted to better uses" (*Tud.* 2.9.8-10). This illustrates how much insight Anne has into both legal and religious matters, designating herself as a participant in the Reformation by using the pronoun "our." Once more disregardful of male authority, she puts Cromwell in his place which certainly must particularly satisfy the female audience. Archbishop Cranmer furthermore emphasizes Anne's significance for the Reformation upon hearing of her arrest. Desperately, he asks Cromwell "Without her is not our Reformation in danger? Was she not our great supporter and advocate?" (*Tud.* 2.9.40-41).

All of the previously mentioned examples indicate that *The Tudors* deliberately reinterprets Anne Boleyn has a central figure in the English Reformation. In that, she resembles powerful women of our time which again underlines the contemporariness in Dormer's Anne Boleyn.

* * *

The religious significance of Anne's character is not the only thing that changes towards the end of season on and beginning of season two. Previously it has been argued that Anne Boleyn is presented as virtuous and chaste, allowing her desire for sexuality only to be displayed in a dream sequence. This gradually changes within the second season of *The Tudors.* Already the final episode of the first season introduces that change (*Tud.* 1.10.45-49). Firstly, Thomas Wyatt, who is bitter about having lost his beloved Anne to the King, brags to his friend, the musician Thomas Tallis, looking at Anne: "For what it's worth, I did fuck her" (*Tud.* 1.10.24). This sheds a completely new light on Anne. The real Anne Boleyn never granted any sexual favours to Thomas Wyatt (Weir 159), but it is a matter of fact that, when she had been at the English court for a year, she and the young nobleman Henry Percy fell in love, which was followed by a secret betrothal. They never married because Wolsey made them break the betrothal, officially for matters of class as Anne had only been a commoner (Lindsey 52). The Henry Percy incident is entirely ignored by *The Tudors.* Instead, the fictionalized Wyatt fulfils the function of both Anne's suitors poet Thomas Wyatt and Henry Percy and merges them into one person. Whether Anne had sexual relations with Percy is not recorded, but Wyatt's statement, expressed in an

44

extremely twenty-first century vulgar slang, suggests that Hirst wants the audience to believe, or at least wonder, that she did so, which then has the effect that the viewer begins to doubt Anne's persistently proclaimed chastity.

Secondly, in the final scene Anne and Henry ride in a dark and foggy forest. A sinister and conspirative mood is created, underlined also by past-paced music. Without exchanging any words, only eager views, they stop and hastily undress each other. Appositely to the wild nature of the forest, the two lovers finally succumb to their own nature. Consumed by their mutual desire, they finally commit sexual intercourse. But Anne, who does not seem the least like a virgin in that scene, pushes Henry away with the words "You mustn't!" before he can finish the act. Both seem extremely frustrated about their unfulfilled physical needs Henry storms off furiously whereas Anne is left lying on the ground while a flashback reveals that she is thinking about the words her father told her in the second episode: "Perhaps you could imagine a way to keep his interest more prolonged?" As final scene of the first season, this scene has the function to keep the audience on the string for the second season, which it magnificently does unfolding the intensity of Anne's and Henry's relationship that is increasingly marked by both desperation and stagnation.

Generally as well as with the regard to the portrayal of Anne Boleyn, the second season is more fast-paced, depicting events of only four years, starting in 1532 (as the initial caption reveals) and ending with Anne Boleyn's execution in May 1536. Dormer explains that the plot lines are now a great deal denser, darker, more serious and rapid. Where her character is concerned, she states that Anne is different in the second season as her psychological and emotional arches are getting much steeper (Dormer, Season 2 Podcast). It is more and more shown how much weight is lying heavy on her shoulders and that it gets increasingly harder for her to carry it. Also, the programme gradually includes moments where Anne behaves in ways that serve to stimulate Henry's later doubts of her fidelity to him, which then eventually lead to her condemnation. In the initial episode of the second season the character of the musician Mark Smeaton (David Alpay), who is later executed along with Anne for allegedly having had sexual intercourse with her, is introduced to her by Thomas Wyatt, who sarcastically congratulates her for reaching so high (*Tud.* 2.1.21-24). She, in return, thanks him and assures him, with a seductive smile, that she will never forget that they once were true friends. Bitterly, he says that he wishes that he could forget that. Then Wyatt introduces Smeaton to her saying: "He likes to be called just plain Mark." Whereupon Anne answers in a very flirtatious manner but at the same time using her quick wit for a play on words, as desirable for the ideal court lady, "how could he possibly be called plain?" She locks eyes with Smeaton as she had done only seconds earlier with Wyatt. In doing so, Dormer once more demonstrates that she is able to use her eyes, although light-blue in colour, in the similar way the actual Anne Boleyn had used her dark eyes on the courtiers. The subsequent effect is that Smeaton seems smitten by the fictionalized Anne. She is also represented to be fascinated by him, but probably only in an artistic way, as she commands him to play the violin for her. Impressed by his talent, she asks him to introduce her to the art of violin-playing. He steps behind her, moving her hands simultaneously along with his, so they appear to be playing the instrument together. This scene reveals how historical accuracy in historical fiction sometimes needs to be bent for artistic purposes. The historical Smeaton was a keyboard player, a virginalist. But certainly teaching to play the violin seems more suitable to be used for representing an overtly flirtatious moment on screen than using a keyboard instrument. Also, the Tudors did not have violins but viols and lutes and Smeaton would not have played an Irish tune, as he does in the scene, at the English court. Apart from these anachronisms, the scene seems heavily contemporized in the way Anne behaves with Smeaton. Although Anne often used sharp words to Henry she always conducted herself royally when social inferiors, as Smeaton had been, were present (Fletcher). But these moments have the purpose to gradually disclose Anne as a seducer rather than the innocent virgin as which she had been portrayed earlier.

This happens in another scene. While on a visit to France in 1532 to renew his friendship with the King of France, it is brought to light to the viewer that when Anne had served at the French court as a young girl, she had not been as virtuous as proclaimed. In a conversation with Francis, Anne asks him in French: "But there are some things, perhaps, which Your Majesty knows about me, which I would rather you kept a secret, and never mention to the King." Francis assures her: "I am a Frenchman. I would never betray the secrets of a woman. Especially a beautiful woman who must naturally have a great many (Tud. 2.2.47-50)." This suggests that Anne indeed has many secrets and her precedent statements about her maidenhead were a lie. Her virtuousness that had been so carefully constructed throughout the first season, with the purpose that the audience perceives Anne through Henry's eyes, gradually begins to crumble.

Anne is more and more exposed as having a dishonest side to her, which normally would lead to a decrease of the audience's sympathies with her character. But this is automatically revoked as Anne is simultaneously depicted in a way that also discloses how difficult it must have been for her to deal with the situations she finds herself in and that she gradually begins to lose it. Francis's statement to Anne about her impending queenship after the hitherto mentioned moments underlines this: "The station you will be asked to occupy is not an easy one, especially to those not born into it. It's much harder to have everything than to have nothing. If I had not been born to be king, I certainly would not have wished this fate upon me." Anne nods acknowledging, with a hint of bitterness in her gaze.

The first time Anne obviously breaks is prior to the scene of her coronation when she is already heavily pregnant for the first time (*Tud.* 2.3.24-26). Her sister Mary comes to see her, and initially, Anne seems really happy and euphoric telling her sister that astrologers have already confirmed that the child will be the longed for son. But while she is excitedly admiring Holbein's designs for the coronation process, her face suddenly and unexpectedly changes to an expression of fear, sadness and desperation. Her sister asks for the reason, but Anne is unable to speak. Anne has gambled everything on giving birth to a boy and in this scene her doubts about being able to do so become for the first time visible for the audience. The pressure that this is exerting on her is immense. And when she, in the final part of this episode, is then delivered of a baby girl, the Princess Elizabeth, she looks devastated, telling Henry, who evidently is frozen in shock, "I'm so sorry!"(*Tud.* 2.3.45-48). The viewer is then aware, also with the certain advantage of hindsight, that this is the moment, which introduces Anne Boleyn's downfall. Alluding greatly to the image of the betrayed wife, the episode concludes with two contrasting images. Firstly, the viewer sees how Henry for the first time since he had met Anne takes a mistress and secondly, Anne sitting in bed still exhausted of having given birth, holding her baby (*Tud.* 2.3.48-49). This is a deeply touching scene, suggesting that Anne will have to walk her remaining path of life alone, without the support of her husband (for that matter, the same argument can be applied to baby Elizabeth). It perhaps can be proposed that this scene, which only lasts a few seconds, rather like a still image, depicts a moment, where the viewer feels the greatest sympathy with Anne Boleyn, right next to her execution scene, because she seems extremely human and vulnerable. It is one of the rare moments in the show, which of course multiply within the course of the second season, when her guard is let down and instead of the sophisticated female courtier, the obeying daughter, the fearless reformist, the passionate lover and wife, an ordinary woman is being depicted, a woman that evokes compassion in the (particularly female) spectators.

It is not documented how deep the maternal bond between Anne and her daughter Elizabeth went, but the series suggests, in accordance to establish Anne as a popular character in *The Tudors*, that she was a very loving mother to Elizabeth during the short time they had together and in the light of the sixteenth century restrictions of the upbringing of royal children. This is corroborated by certain recorded occurrences in that context that the producers consciously chose to portray, for instance that the historical Anne Boleyn wanted to breastfeed the baby Elizabeth. Together with her ladies-in-waiting, the new mother Anne cares for her daughter. Anne begins to unbutton her dress. At this moment, Henry enters demanding to know what she is doing. Confidently, she replies: "May I not feed her from my own breast?" Taking Elizabeth away from Anne, he tells her that it is unsuitable for queens to do that and this task is only reserved to the wet nurse. Anne reluctantly obeys (*Tud.* 2.4.11-13). In our time, it is absolutely normal to breastfeed one's own child and in intentionally selecting to depict Anne's attempt to do so, *The Tudors* again manages to illustrate the very modern traits of Anne Boleyn.

The birth of Elizabeth marks the beginning of Anne's downfall. From then on, Anne's character is presented in two ways. On the one hand, she is increasingly depicted as arrogant, cold and proud, thus in a dislikeable manner. But on the other hand, this is then again deconstructed as it is simultaneously shown how much she has to endure and suffer and what pressure she is under. The fifth episode of the second season is, for example, representative of this. In one of the initial scenes Anne, pregnant for the second time, proudly walks through the royal halls to her chamber, evidently enjoying that everyone is bowing before her, referring to her as "Your Majesty". Seconds after, she cramps, breaks down and loses the baby, which evidently devastates her. Pale and depressed, she is lying in bed. Henry, also grief struck, comes to see her only to tell her that there will not be a public announcement. Instead of comforting his wife, he leaves her alone with her sorrow and sense of failure (*Tud.* 2.5.7-9). Then even more pressure is put on Anne by her father who accuses her of having killed the baby. He threatens her: "From now on we must all be careful, you especially, not to lose the King's love. Or everything is lost. Everything. For all of us." A close up of Anne's terrified face reveals that she begins to realize how high the stakes are for her (*Tud.* 2.5.11-13). A later scene then shows her dancing with Smeaton, artificially laughing trying to keep up appearances and to ignore her miscarriage. But soon after, Anne is depicted alone in her chambers, sitting in front of a mirror looking at her face while she is drinking wine. She appears deranged and on the verge to insanity. She sends for her brother George to confide in him that she is afraid that Henry, with his now absolute power, could still, regardless of the Act of Succession, make Mary queen above Elizabeth. She swears that she knows that "she is my death and I am hers" (*Tud.* 2.5.24-29).

Anne's paranoia grows with every episode knowing that Henry has more affairs. She even believes that he keeps a harem somewhere with all of his women. As every other woman would be, she is hurt and jealous that Henry is obviously betraying her. She is sure that something is going to happen to her since, as she mentions, there is a prophecy that a queen of England will be burnt. And she is unable to give the King a son (*Tud.* 2.6.26-28). It is not certain whether this prophecy existed or not but *The Tudors* uses this possibility to evoke an awareness in Anne that her life might be in danger. Anne realizes that all is breaking apart for her when she interrogates Henry about his mistresses. He forbids her to speak, but she gainsays him again, exclaiming that they once swore to be truthful to each other as this was Henry's professed definition of true love. Henry no longer having a love-clouded mind tells her what the truth is: "You must shut your eyes and endure. Like your betters have done before you." And he threatens her that he can drag her down as fast as he has raised her and that he regrets having married her. Clearly Henry's love has turned into hate and Anne is now aware of that (*Tud.* 2.6.43-45). What Henry admired in Anne as a mistress, he cannot accept in her as a wife. Her outspokenness and temper increasingly infuriate him. Even her brother reminds Anne that she is the Queen of England and that she should act like it. She should behave more like Queen Katherine not betraying her feelings to everyone and seem happy despite her misery (*Tud.* 2.6.7-9). But Anne cannot endure her ordeal silently, thus the audience sees her increasingly breaking apart. Generally, Dormers performance of Anne Boleyn in the second season has gained more depth as opposed to the first one. In an newspaper article it has been suggested that "Dormer was a weak link in the in the first season [...]. But as her story progresses and Anne's position becomes more tenuous, Dormer's vulnerability comes to the fore, and the portrayal begins to make sense" (Bianco).

What is noticeable is that Anne's misery is in several instances very similar to Katherine's. Suggesting the repetitiveness of history, Hirst intentionally gives Anne phrases once associated with Henry's first wife (Wray 53), as for instance, "I am the King's true wedded wife (*Tud.* 2.9.39)," "If I had a son it would bring about a golden world (*Tud.* 2.7.35)," or "Will you come to my bed tonight? (*Tud.* 2.6.9)". Also that Henry begins to take a fancy in Anne's lady-in-waiting Jane Seymour (Anita Briem) for whom he then discards Anne evokes the circularity of history.

Anne miscarries for the second time after accidentally having found her husband in a private moment with Jane Seymour. In a very intense scene it is revealed that the baby was a boy whereupon Henry furiously accuses Anne: "You've lost my boy!" Desperately Anne cries that he has no one but himself to blame for the miscarriage, that she was so distressed to see him with Jane Seymour. In a little, sad voice she says: "It broke my heart to see you loved others" (*Tud.* 2.8.345-48). It is hard not to feel any empathy for *The Tudors*' interpretation of Anne Boleyn, especially after that scene. This moment portrays in

49

an convincing intensity how painful it must have been for Anne to feel her husband's once passionate love for her to cool, to be aware that he sleeps with other women and, additionally, to suffer from miscarriages without being comforted by anyone. Any other woman, contemporary or not, would be devastated, thus her misery must seems very comprehensible for the audience.

After the second miscarriage, Anne's fate is sealed. Henry is now sure that he had been seduced by witchcraft and a plot against Anne is forged. No longer indestructible, in contrast to the fictionalized assassination attempts, history takes its path and Anne is sentenced to death. Like the historical Anne Boleyn, her fictionalized character retrieves her old countenance carrying herself with honour and dignity, as she once had been admired for. The execution scene is re-staged with attention to accurate historical detail and serves as a fantastic climax of the final episode of the second season. The very last scene, after Anne's execution, is particularly meaningful in terms of metaphorical analysis. Prior to Anne's condemnation, several times Henry can be seen watching a pair of two white swans swimming in the pond of the royal gardens. While doing so, Henry appears melancholic and sorrowful. The audience automatically assumes that Henry grieves the failed relationship and marriage to Anne, whom he once passionately and truly loved. The two swans, majestic in their appearance as well as being birds that mate for life and cannot live without each other, stand to symbolize Anne and Henry. Especially, when the viewer remembers the pageant where they meet for the first time and Anne wears a white ballet dress in which she looks like a swan. Due to the impression of Henry's melancholy, the viewer still sees Henry in a positive light although his treatment of Anne and the series' clear portrayal of Anne of being innocent of the charges against her might suggest otherwise. In the very last scene, however, Henry is shown sitting at the end of a long table. A dozen of his servants bring him a massive, covered tray. It is not digressive to think that Anne's head might be placed underneath the cover. But as the cover is lifted one of the two swans lies stuffed on the tray being used as the surrounding decoration of a pie. While everyone applauds, Henry breaks off one of the swan's wings and greedily devours the pie with his bare hands and a maniacal gaze in his eyes (*Tud.* 2.10.44-46). Without doubt, the swan symbolizes Anne's downfall and death for which Henry is made responsible when interpreting the swan metaphor. Heralding an outlook for the subsequent season, Henry is now consciously portrayed as the monster he is to become. In opposition to the timeless and eternal theme of "happily-ever-after" this anti-happy end contributes to *The Tudors* portrayal of Anne Boleyn as a victim, a victim of the male-dominated Tudor world. At the beginning, she is forced to ensnare Henry by her father and uncle, as their puppet to denounce Wolsey and to secure family fortunes. Then Henry persistently assures her that he will get annulment to marry her. Anne patiently waits. And in the end, once the King has obtained what he wanted, failing to bear him a male heir, his passion for her begins to diminish. To get rid of her, he instructs Cromwell to construct a case against her. Of course, despite her victimization, Anne is not illustrated as a weak or flawless character. Certainly, she has her short-comings but she nevertheless mostly evokes sympathy with the audience. Dormer's Anne Boleyn clearly appeals to a twenty-first century audience. This can certainly be explained by the fact that she was a woman well ahead of her time, as often has been claimed. The British historian David Starkey, for instance, identifies "Anne Boleyn and her daughter, Elizabeth I, as being honourary men of their times." He furthermore expounds that Anne Boleyn used "her education, her intelligence, her instincts and her style to outweigh the disadvantage of her gender during that era. Anne Boleyn is an intriguing character. She seems to appeal to modern-day women in a very potent way. Because she was such an independently opinionated and spirited young woman, which at the time was unheard of" (Strachan). Thus, this very emotionally engaging portrayal of Anne Boleyn in *The Tudors* presents and re-imagines her as the tragic heroine of the first two seasons, and the fact that Anne Boleyn was an advanced female for her time supports her very contemporized depiction.

4. Fine Feathers Make Fine Birds: Anne Boleyn and the Mediality of Costume

Next to the set, it is also the costume that works as an instrument to create a sense of pastness in an historical film. Nevertheless, no matter how historically correct the reconstruction of historical dress in a film might be, the present is always referenced in them. Historians and ethnologists consider this as an ethnocentric back projection, but in the film business it is the basic rule that the contemporary cultural environment is determining in the production of a film. The overall task of historical costumes on screen simply is to establish a visual and cultural connection to the current perception. This contemporariness in costume rarely is detrimental to the quality of the film (Devoucoux 125-28). These criteria are by all means applicable to the costumes of *The Tudors*, particularly to the costumes of Dormer's Anne Boleyn. It has previously been argued that *The Tudors'* portrayal of Anne Boleyn is a rather contemporized one, which is, if nothing else, noticeable in her costume(s). Furthermore, the depiction of Anne Boleyn's social rise from a commoner to queen is also reflected in her dresses. These will be the two main points of focus for this chapter.

The Tudors costume designer Joan Bergin, who won two sequent Emmy Awards for her telegenic, opulent costumes, has stated that she is "forever searching to interpret with a modern sensibility but still keep seventy per cent of what's correct for Tudor time" (Rochlin). Certainly, the costume designs were influenced by the contemporary necessity of sexiness and desirability in film, and this is a matter which Bergin kept in mind when reinterpreting early modern English clothes. She aspired "a sexy modern Tudor look," justifying this with the fact that in Tudor times, in contrast to "Victorian morality, where women couldn't show their ankles [...] ladies went to court to find a husband" (Hohenadel), hence they needed to visually appeal to the male courtiers. Her primary intention was for the clothes to speak to a modern audience rather than to appear strange and outlandish. As a result, she took Tudor garments and added touches that allow for modern correspondence (TV New Zealand).

So, when studying authentic Tudor dress, it immediately becomes clear that the costumes in *The Tudors* are modernized, that is made sexier and more attractive than their historical counterparts. Image 07 shows Anne Boleyn in a scene from the Field of the Cloth of Gold. What is particularly striking is that Anne does not wear any headgear, which is extremely unusual for Tudor women. The respectable Tudor woman had her head covered as "depictions of bare heads, disordered dress or nakedness signalled distraction, madness or poverty (Mikhaila and Malcolm-Davies 10). Although it was decreed by St Paul that women's hair had to be covered, unbound hair was accepted for girls who had not yet

53

been married. But still, this revealed a lack of discipline or mischievous intent. Surely, during the Field of Cloth of Gold, Anne was yet unmarried but it seems unlikely that she would have had her hair uncovered, especially on an occasion like the Field of Cloth of Gold, a display of wealth and richness, when in the sixteenth century the garments of a person revealed their financial and spiritual worth (Mikhaila and Malcolm-Davies 10). Also Anne Boleyn is always associated with the French hood. For the fashionable Tudor woman the principle type of headgear was the hood. She is known for having introduced the French hood at the English court which had a rounded top rather than the gable point, which was characteristic of the English hood (Mikhaila and Malcolm-Davies 28). In *The Tudors* Anne Boleyn is never shown wearing either a typical French or English hood. In a some episodes (2.4., 2.7., 2.9.) there are a few occurrences when she is wearing a seemingly modernized version of a French hood that is elevated from the head, more like a coronet, and without an attached veil that covers the woman's hair. The only exception where Anne is wearing a traditional or accurate version of a French hood is one scene when Henry looks at a mini portrait of Anne in a locket (*Tud.* 2.5.19) which is analogical in style with the Hever Castle portrait of Anne. In this mini portrait, Dormer's Anne Boleyn looks truly Early Modern, wearing a French hood where only a little bit of her hairline with middle parting is showing and the hood is closely fitted to the head. It is the only time throughout the series that Anne Boleyn looks that traditionally Tudoresque. As in the Hever Castle portrait, Anne is wearing her famous "B" necklace, a detail that has also been considered for both the scene of image 07 and the one with the her father and the falcon. This necklace is an exact replica of her original necklace, and what is interesting is that this necklace became so popular due to Anne's character wearing it, that it can now be bought in various jewellery stores where it can be purchased in every letter, as Bergin explains (Royal Stylemakers 3). So, Anne Boleyn did not only set a trend at the English court with the French hood but also in the twenty-first century with her famous necklace. Again the boundaries between past and present are blurred. As already mentioned, throughout the seasons Anne is never portrayed wearing a hood which contributes to the argument how modernized *The Tudors'* costumes are. Although she wears all different kinds of head pieces, which of course become more opulent the more power she gains, there is very often emphasis on displaying her dark-brown, long hair. Even though the French hood does not seem as conservative as the English hood as it allows for more hairline to be revealed, to our modern eye uncovered, healthy, long hair is more appealing and attractive. So to even put more emphasis on the beauty of Anne's hair, instead of covering it up with hoods, often her hair is decorated with coronets and crowns, especially in the second season, or diadems ornamented with jewels and pearls (see images 08 and 09). Like this, she appears a great deal more modern and adapted to twenty-first century style.

Contributing to the modern need of desirability in film characters, also sometimes her costumes seem to reveal more flesh than appropriate for the time portrayed. In episode three, four and six of the first season, when she is at her family residence Hever Castle and Henry begins his courtship of her, she wears a off-the-shoulder, cream coloured dress, imprinted with large red flowers (see image 10). Showing one's bare shoulder is very atypical for Tudor times. The first time Anne wears this dress, which can for the following reasons be called the 'Hever Castle dress', when she is lying on a meadow at Hever Castle together with Wyatt (*Tud.* 1.3.20), then in the subsequent episode, still at Hever reading one of Henry's letter to her brother George (*Tud.* 1.4.22), and once more at Hever with her father and uncle (*Tud.* 1.6.3). Again, she respectively is wearing her hair unbound and without any sort of headgear. Of course, in these three scenes she is not in public but at her family residence which could be the reason for that. In the second scene, however, the bare shoulders have a great effect when she puts her hair behind her back to show George the lavish necklace with a cross pendant adorned with a white pearl, which Henry gave to her. One might also suggest that, as the naked shoulders rather emphasize Anne's delicate neck, this is an ironic allusion to her later fate. On the whole, this dress lets Anne appear very young and girlish which is certainly not suitable to attract the attention of the King. Therefore, when Anne is shown at court, her dresses seem more precious and graceful. She often wears her lady-in-waiting dress (image 11) which is similar in style to the dresses of her fellow ladies-in-waiting, with the difference that Anne never wears a hood as the other ladies do, probably to make her stand out from the other "ordinary" girls. What is, however, noticeable here is that most ladies-in-waiting wear an atifet, a French hood with a heart-shaped crescent, which became only popular with the reign of Mary Queen of Scots (Women's Dress, *Tudors Wiki*). Visually, this kind of headgear is more flattering than the French or the English hood, as it does not conceal to much of the woman's hair and head. That is supposedly the reason why this anachronism has found its way into Henry VIII.'s court, reinterpreted in *The Tudors*.

Another costume of Anne's that is remarkably contemporary in contrast to Tudor dress code is the white ballet-dancer/swan inspired dress that she is wearing in the pageant when Henry first notices her (image 12). Although it is extremely eye-catching, which certainly was the purpose of the dress in that scene; it is highly inaccurate, historically speaking. As already mentioned, showing that much flesh in Tudor times, even during a pageant, was extremely unlikely. To adopt this dress to Tudor standards of fashion, Anne at least would have had to wear long bell-shaped or trumpet sleeves. Furthermore, the dress is slightly see-through which is a very modern-day trait for clothes but definitely not suitable for the sixteenth century. This dress appears more like underwear than a costume. Bergin explains that her intention in designing this dress was to take a ballet dress and to reinterpret it as Tudor. In its basic, the dress is a creation of the designer label Balenciaga which had been inspired by the Elizabethan Age (Royal Stylemakers 1). Bergin obviously kept the Elizabethan theme by providing Anne also with a neck ruff. So in total, this dress is melange of contemporary and Elizabethan dress, not the least adapted to the style of the 1520s and 1530s. But this does not influence the scene negatively. The subtext of this scene was to illustrate how Anne caught Henry's eye and to make the effect she had on men understandable for a twenty-first century audience, hence this rather revealing and noticeable dress was designed for Anne.

Another scene illustrates Anne in a dress that also seems very contemporarily touched. Image 13 shows Anne and Henry during a dance at court. It is from the same episode, when Henry offers Anne to be his 'maîtresse en titre', a few scenes prior to the dance. This dress seems more like a nightgown or a modern-day summers dress inspired by the Seventies, than a sixteenth century court gown. But it in its girlish and virginal design, suitably in white, the colour of innocence, it sends out the message that Anne still is a virgin and wants to keep her virginity and that she is not willing and too virtuous to merely become Henry's mistress.

Anne Boleyn's costume is also very remarkable in terms of contemporariness in *The Tudors*', when she goes on a riding and picnic trip with her royal lover (*Tud.* 1.6.24). Under her black gown and dark purple cloak, Anne is wearing breeches and knee high black leather boots. Firstly, breeches were only reserved for men and secondly the ordinary shoe for both Tudor men and women were not knee high boots but robust high-fitting ankle boots without heels (Mikhaila and Malcolm-Davies 33). However, Anne Boleyn was not an ordinary woman and this is the way in which Bergin re-imagined Anne Boleyn. She explains that she wanted to illustrate how sassy she was. So the breeches and the boots, also made by a modern-day designer label, were chosen to make her look more outrageous and modern (Royal Stylemakers 1). As much as this costume may appear historically inaccurate, it nevertheless stresses Anne's extraordinariness and her progressive character. What is also striking in that scene is that this is the first time that Anne and Henry wear matching outfits. This can be interpreted as symbol of their increasing affection for each other. Suitably, the title of this episode is 'True Love'. In this episode, Henry gradually shows his affection for Anne openly and publicly: at first on a picnic with his friends, then later in the episode at court. After that, a series of Anne and Henry wearing matching clothes follows. The first time they are wearing matching clothes at court is in the episode that narrates the events of 1528/1529, as the opening scene shows Cardinal Campeggio's arrival at the English court as a papal legate which historically happened in October 1528 (Weir 189-90). Henry is in the middle of his attempt to obtain an annulment of his marriage to Katherine of Aragon on the grounds that she had already been married to his brother Arthur. Everyone at court is now aware that Henry's passion for Anne is not elusive but that he seriously wants to marry her. During the court festivity Henry and Anne are both dressed in light-gold garments to underline that they belong together. Around them, all the courtiers are discussing the King's 'Great Matter' while glancing at Anne and Henry in disbelief. Firstly, Thomas More is portrayed conversing with Cardinal Campeggio, then the latter discusses the matter with ambassador Mendoza. Henry's sister openly demonstrates her resentfulness of Anne Boleyn towards her brother calling her a "cheap nothing". Subsequently, Anne (again wearing no headgear on her unbound hair) and Henry dance and truly appear like an harmonious couple, no less because of their synchronized costumes (*Tud.* 1.8.17-22). They appear again completely synchronized in dress in the following episode. The King's entrance is announced and he enters, leading Anne by the hand both dressed in majestically, bejewelled golden-reddish outfits. Additionally, Anne is this time wearing a crown-like, lavish, gemmed headpiece. Although still in the middle of the validity suit, Anne gives the impression of being queen already. In the next scene, the purpose of this stately entrance is revealed by Henry telling Anne: "Did you see? They were all looking at you. I'm glad. I want them to look at you. I want them to be envious. I want all of them to know exactly how much I love you" (*Tud.* 1.9.7-10). Costume on screen, or on stage, always functions as a tool of communication with a certain objective (Mikhaila and Malcolm-Davies 10). Here, in that scene, with the costumes Bergin clearly aimed to deliver the message that assertively Anne and Henry will be husband and wife, at any cost. In terms of Tudors style, Anne's gown is partly accurate. For women, the triangular shape was aspired as opposed to the square shape of men. In that respect, both Anne's and Henry's costume are accurate. What is also accurate is that Anne's gown is square-necked, yet her tight-fitted sleeves are anachronistic. In the Henrician period it was the prerogative of the noblefolk to have large sleeves as those would have been impractical for anyone who had to work manually. For ladies, especially trumpet or bell-shaped sleeves were fashionable.

What also hints at Bergin's modern interpretation of Tudor dress is the fact that the characteristic multi-layers of a garment is missing, probably for practical reasons, too. There is no hint that Anne wears a petticoat and kirtle underneath her gown, as a Tudor woman would have, as this would have been visible at the neckline. But concerning its shape, the dress is very Tudoresque as the bodice for the upper body part is tightly fitted whereas the gown of lower body part was full and wide. The shape of the skirt suggests that Anne is also wearing a farthingale underneath, a construction which holds the skirts away from the body, typical for women's clothing of the era (Mikhaila and Malcolm-Davies 20-22).

There are various other occasions where Anne and Henry are dressed in harmonizing clothes. One is the opening scene of season two where Anne and Henry are depicted in church, praying (*Tud.* 2.1.2). Both are wearing black, pious, high-necked garments. Anne looks particularly conservative in that scene and it might be the most unattractive costume the observer will ever see her dressed in on *The Tudors*. They also match their clothes in a court festivity (*Tud.* 2.2.26), both dressed in golden, cream-coloured dresses, after the submission of the clergy has been implemented and Henry tells Anne that he will invest her with the title Marquess of Pembroke, and also afterwards when Anne is eventually made Marquess of Pembroke (*Tud.* 2.2.32). Henry and Anne are both wearing rich golden cloth decorated with white pearls during Anne's coronation (*Tud.* 2.3.30). This is the last time the royal couple is depicted in matching outfits as a few scenes after the coronation Anne gives birth, not to the expected male heir, but to a baby girl. That indicates how Henry and Anne are increasingly distancing themselves from each other. Henry is no longer faithful to Anne and starts taking mistresses again, Anne miscarries for the first time and becomes increasingly distempered with Henry and cries often. Interestingly, it has been recorded that the real Anne and Henry both dressed similarly during the court ball that was held on the occasion of Katherine of Aragon's death in January 1536. They both dressed in the colour yellow, the colour of royal mourning in Spain (Weir 299). But in the equivalent scene on *The Tudors*, only Anne is dressed in yellow (*Tud.* 2.7.48). That suggests that the producers of the show probably considered matching outfits misleading with regard to Anne's and Henry's relationship as this would hint at a momentary romantic revitalization of the royal couple. Throughout the series, their matching clothes symbolized their romantic and spiritual unity, their mutual love for each other, but at this point in the programme this is no longer applicable. Only few scenes before, Jane Seymour had been introduced to the show with Henry showing obvious interest in her. As a result, even though this occurrence is historically inaccurate, it serves a certain purpose in reinterpreting the Tudors. Also, the importance of costume in communicating a particular message is exemplary in this depiction.

That Anne and Henry begin to wear matching costumes as their relationship becomes more serious, also has the purpose to demonstrate Anne's social rise. Bergin explains that they intended the costumes to reflect the characters' changing fortunes and Anne Boleyn is a very good example for that. Her costumes develop more than those of any other protagonist of the show. Her dresses become more elegant and elaborate so that they eventually match the King's clothes by the end of season one. Anne evolves from a young girl who is being disdained by the other courtiers for being an opportunist to a grandiose, impressive, influential woman that many people admire. *The Tudors'* costume designer states that the achievement of this transformation has not been easy in terms of creating the costumes as many costumes had to be made from scratch. Fabrics as well as already existing dresses were gathered from all over the world. It is noticeable that some costumes from a 1930s Erol Flynn film served as particularly useful for *The Tudors* as they had been wonderfully crafted with great attention to detail. Anne's coronation dress for example had been made from 150 years old hand-spun silver material, which they found in a London shop. Bergin emphasizes the importance of costume in *The Tudors,* since, with the stress on character as typical for contemporary American television shows, the costumes proved as essential in terms of a character's personal evolution. Bergin attempted to visually develop every character through their clothing. It is Anne's costumes that contribute a great deal to the audience's understanding of her transformation from a young, inexperienced daddy's girl into a magnificent queen. The format of the television series allows for such a conversion in terms of costume design. In a two-hour feature film, Anne would have had no more than three 'set-piece' dresses, but in *The Tudors* there are at least one or two for each episode. In total, Dormer's Anne Boleyn had about 17 major costumes including head pieces, jewels and shoes, which all had been newly designed and created.[14] The result is that "in gigantic jewels and plunging necklines, she [Anne Boleyn] becomes progressively more stunning as the series unfolds and her power over Henry expands" (*Time,* "When Royals Became Rockstars"). The plunging necklines, however, are not exactly accurate. During the first two decades of the sixteenth century, it was still a lady's common habit to make her bosom's curves visible beneath the bodice. But from the 1520s on, the clothing for women appeared to be stiffer and the curves less

---

14 Different interviews with Joan Bergin from "The Royal Stylemakers 1" and from "*The Tudors –* Costume Designer Joan Bergin" *Television New Zealand* as well as "The Tudor Costumes: Anne Boleyn" on *The Tudors Wiki.*

obvious, as contemporary portraits and paintings suggest (Mikhaila and Malcolm-Davies 22). Yet, making a lady's curves visible clearly contributes to her attractiveness and is thus welcomed as an attribute to be displayed on the contemporary television screen. At any rate, Anne Boleyn's metamorphosis in the context of clothing is outstanding and a comparison between image 14 and images 15 and 16 stresses this point. Image 14 is from the very first time Anne Boleyn is presented in the series, as her father comes home to tell Anne and Mary that they are going to attend the Field of Cloth of Gold (see chapter 2). With this puff-sleeved, plain dress, Anne truly looks unspectacular and girlish, especially with her unbound, long and curly hair. Image 15 depicts Anne during a feast for the French ambassador (season two, episode six) and image 16 is from her execution scene in the final episode of season two. The difference between Anne as a young girl and Anne later as (the condemned) Queen Of England is immense. Her hair neatly put up, accentuated with a coronet, her pearl necklace, pearl earrings, the way she graciously holds the silver wine goblet and her elegant, majestic dress represent her as a credible, worthy Queen of England. The contrast to image 15 is evident. Even during her execution Anne is still portrayed as a refined and magnificent queen dressed in a ravishing, rich Tudor gown.

Her social rise reflected in costume is yet not detrimental to the contemporariness in her clothing that is so important for the costume designer Bergin, as she has stressed. Many costumes are influenced by the Elizabethan Age, but some dresses also have very modern-day attributes, which the following examples will prove. Image 17 depicts a furious Anne Boleyn running after her husband whom she thinks to run off to one of his mistresses. While she is pacing through the royal halls, Brereton has an assassination dream sequence, where he sees himself stabbing Anne to death (season two, episode six). Anne's costume in these sequences seems rather misplaced with regard to typical sixteenth century dress. With the high-necked collar, the dress's transparent upper part and the shiny fabric, this dress appears like a melange of Edwardian, Gothic and modern-day ball gowns. The beige coat adds to the costumes contemporariness, too. With her unrestrained curly hair, she gives the impression of an enraged witch. But that is exactly the image which was aspired to represent Anne in this scene. Brereton, in his religious fanaticism, imagines Anne exactly like this, a distempered, evil witch that wants to lead the country into eternal condemnation. Furthermore, her unruly and impulsive behaviour in the subsequent accusations of Henry riding out to enjoy himself with his mistresses is underlined by this unusual costume since Anne's conduct is extremely unusual for women of the time. The short sleeves of Anne's costume in image 18 are also anachronistic. Yet, having Anne reveal more skin as appropriate for Tudor times (remembering what nakedness symbolized in the era) resonates with the scene's dark and wild atmosphere (season two, episode seven). Anne is already aware that Henry's affection for her has almost vanished but during a court festivity the royal couple engage in a passionate, lustful dance that appears more like a danced fight. Subsequently, the frenzied fight is consigned to the royal bed with a see-saw who is on top, where they are shown for the last time being intimate with each other, resulting in Anne's last pregnancy. Another example of a sense of contemporariness and "sexy modern Tudor look" is Anne's costume in image 19 during a Christmas celebration at court. The slit down her bodice revealing more cleavage as typical of the time is neither convenient for a Tudor queen nor for the celebration of a religious holiday like Christmas.

The various colours of Anne Boleyn's robes also play a crucial role in representing her rise to power, her fall from grace and also the general atmosphere of situations. In the sixteenth century, the range of colour in clothing was not as various as it is nowadays. Dying was a huge professional industry and the more extraordinary the colour, achieved by complicated dying processes, the more valuable a garment. The main colours thus were white, black, red and blue. The majority of clothes for both women and men was of black colour, whereas true black was difficult to dye, which added to the desirability to wear black. Thus, true black was a colour worn by the richer people of Tudor England. White was also a colour of the fashionable and rich since the white silks of the wealthy were expensive and highly impractical. The sumptuary laws are necessary to mention in the context of Tudor clothing. These were laws that dictated the consumption of goods according to the consumer's respective social class. For example, the sumptuary laws of 1533 decreed that blue and crimson velvet was only reserved for the nobility and garter knights. Generally, red was the colour of the ordinary woman while blue was a man's colour. Mainly middling and fashionable people widely wore other colours. It has to be noticed that vivid colours could be created by the natural dyes of the time but the nuances were not as saturated as those of modern-day fashion. The colour purple held a special position in the Tudor Age. It was extremely expensive to create, especially in grain silk and therefore only the immediate royal family was reserved to wear it, according to the statute of 1533 (Mikhaila and Malcolm-Davies 39-41). This is a nice detail that has been used in *The Tudors*. Anne Boleyn, now feeling herself to be de facto queen but still three years away of becoming de jure queen, enters court wearing the colour purple (*Tud.* 1.10.13-15). Several courtiers are appalled by her indecency whereupon Anne openly denounces Katherine saying "I care nothing for Katherine. I would rather see her hanged than acknowledge her as my mistress." Anne intentionally wears a purple dress and a crown-like headpiece to let the entire court know that she now belongs to the royal family. This demonstrates again her self-confidence blended with arrogance that contributes to her often polarizing character.

The colour of Anne's costumes with regard to her rise in power is also remarkable. During the first season, Anne's costumes are not yet that extravagant as they will later be. This is also the case for the range of colours in her costumes. In the first half of the season, Anne mostly wears gowns in the ordinary colours of the time, that is black, red or crimson, grey and white (as in the pageant). The first shift in her status is illustrated when Henry presents Anne to Wolsey uncovering to him the reason for seeking an annulment by telling him that he intends to marry Anne Boleyn (*Tud.* 1.6.50-52). In that scene, she wears a shiny light-blue silk dress, appearing all the more majestic with an oversized, lavishly bejewelled coronet. Blue being a Tudor colour for men might suggest that Henry now considers Anne as his equal in the decision-making of his 'great matter'. Also, in general, light-blue appears to be a very cold colour which emphasizes Anne playing the ice-queen in front of Wolsey who once called her a "silly girl". In the second season, she also wears an ultramarine blue dress which arguably symbolizes her emotional coldness in the context of her being in a state of shock or distress. Once, for example, when she is furious with Henry for not having Katherine completely abandoned from his life, in the initial episode of the second season, then after her first failed pregnancy in episode five, and again in episode nine after her second miscarriage, evoked by the consternation of seeing Henry kissing Jane Seymour. *The Tudors* costume designer also seems to have been familiar with the sumptuary laws as Anne is dressed in a magnificent crimson velvet gown when she is made Marquess of Pembroke, now officially belonging to the nobility (*Tud.* 2.2.30). Generally, concerning her social elevation, the variety of Anne's dresses' colours becomes greater. As the King's lover and then wife, she now has the means to afford and to be provided with dresses in the most vivid and extraordinary colours. However, when she is gradually falling from Henry's grace, her costumes are becoming increasingly darker and more sinister, especially in the last third of season two after Jane Seymour has been brought to court. Anne is aware of having lost Henry's love and their alienation from each other, therefore the costume designer no longer re-imagines Anne wearing vibrant colours, but darker ones to reflect her soul and to foreshadow her impending doom.

To conclude this chapter on Anne Boleyn's costumes, it furthermore needs to be mentioned that her social rise, reflected in "an escalation of spectacular costumes and a dazzling assortment of "crown-like" headpieces" is portrayed in a direct contrast to "Katherine's gradual descent into poverty, obscurity and illness [...] registered in her increasingly shroud-like clothing" (Wray 42). Image 20 (of Katherine of Aragon) and image 21 (of Anne Boleyn) are from the same scene in season one episode six (the same episode where Anne is later dressed in a light-blue gown when Wolsey enters). Here, the Queen, Katherine of Aragon, enters the royal halls in a very queenly manner being dressed in a luxurious gown wearing a bedecked golden crown-like hairpiece. Anne, still only being a servant to Katherine, is depicted in great contrast to her. Humbly and modestly dressed in an unspectacular dark gown and a girlish hair-band, Anne submissively has to bow as Katherine passes her. But in the second season the tables have turned and it is Anne who looks like a queen whereas Katherine's clothing has become less luxurious and simple as image 22 reveals. This is a still image from a scene of the last minutes of the first episode of season two where Katherine is leaving for the More, as she is finally banished from court by Henry and has been ordered to return the official jewels of the Queens of England. This signifies her unofficial dismissal of her being the Queen of England; hence she is no longer depicted in lavish robes accentuated with rich jewellery.

To sum up, the costumes of Anne Boleyn in *The Tudors* are rarely historically accurate with both its contemporary and many Elizabethan influences. This, however, is not disadvantageous to portraying Anne's rise to power reflected by her costumes which are becoming increasingly more extravagant and more colourful. Also, Anne is represented as a fashionable woman (a point that will be taken up and elaborated on in the subsequent chapter) which is the reason that her costumes might have been more extraordinary and progressive. At any rate, costume designer Joan Bergin successfully managed to realize her concept of creating Tudor costumes with a modern sensibility and that is why these costumes are so fascinating. As they are not one-hundred per cent accurate of the period, the viewer might often think that he or she would like to wear a similar piece her/himself. As a result, some prominent characteristics of Tudor clothing, such as doublets, bodices and ruffs, had found their way into the designer fashion collections of labels such as Chanel and Dolce & Gabbana in autumn 2009. A year before, designer label John Galliano had also dedicated an entire collection to the Tudor dynasty and English designer Gareth Pugh had glamourized the catwalks in Paris with Tudor influenced fashion (La Ferla). This proves that again, the Tudor Era is reinterpreted in contemporary terms, as are the "fine feathers" of Dormer's Anne Boleyn.

5. Anne, a Woman of Our Age: How Kate, Diana and Carrie Do Compare

When Hirst was approached by Showtime to work as the screenwriter for *The Tudors*, they told him what style they had in mind for the series. Therefore, they urged Hirst to study episodes of *The West Wing* (1999-2006), an American television series about life behind the scenes of the White House which portrays politics in an entertaining way (James, "President's Quips"), and to re-imagine *The Tudors* as a sort of *The Sopranos* (1999-2007), a popular American television series centred around Mafia boss Tony Soprano and his family (James, "Horse Heads") set in sixteenth century England with Henry being the patriarch (Hohenadel). This makes the pretensions of contemporariness in *The Tudors* already evident. But these television series are not the only ones that have parallels to modern-day American television shows. Wray's title of her essay concerning *The Tudors* already hints at the programme *Desperate Housewives* (2004, still running) using similar structures to create and depict their female characters that are the narrative's main concern. Also, it can be argued that particularly Dormer's Anne Boleyn combines character traits of the four female lead characters of HBO's controversial series *Sex and the City* (1998-2004). But *The Tudors'* contemporized Anne Boleyn does not only have parallels with fictional women of the twentieth or the twenty-first century but also with popular real life women. Therefore, to close the circle, this final chapter of the thesis once more attempts to focus on the contemporariness of *The Tudors'* Anne Boleyn in terms of determining associations with modern-day women, both fictional and non-fictional.

In the press, the long-term girlfriend of Prince William, second in line to the succession to English throne, Kate Middleton is dubbed 'Waity Katie'. Kate has been in a relationship with the man who will one day become King of England for almost eight years. Yet, despite of persistent speculations of the media of an upcoming engagement, the prince is reluctant to make Kate his royal wife. Of course, Henry had not been reluctant to marry Anne, the reasons for that were different. Yet, she had been in the waiting line for several years, just like 'Waity Katie', who is still keeps on waiting (*Krone* and Wordsworth). But this is not the only parallel between these two women who hold/held the love an English (future) king. Just by her sheer physical appearance, Kate Middleton could also have been cast as Anne Boleyn in *The Tudors*. She is beautiful, has long dark hair and a slender frame. Also the way she got the Prince's attention is astonishingly similar. Instead of becoming hysterical and overly eager to impress William, as most girls are likely to do when meeting one of the world's most eligible bachelors, Kate retained her composure and dignity while exuding calm self-confidence. In this she appeared rather unique and extraordinary, which were factors which stirred Prince William's interest in the young woman. It is exactly in this manner how *The Tudors*' Anne Boleyn is portrayed when meeting Henry for the first time, and thus manages to attract his attention. Additionally, Kate Middleton is said to be courteous, mentally strong and also enjoys dancing and partying in night clubs, a twenty-first century equivalent to court festivities which both the fictional and the historical Anne Boleyn took much delight in (Brook).

Furthermore, Kate's mother Carole Middleton has taken over Thomas Boleyn's and Norfolk's job in pushing her daughter to become a royal girlfriend. Like Thomas Boleyn who instructs his daughter to "put yourself in his way" (*Tud.* 1.3.40) "Meddling Middleton," as she is referred to by some of William's friends, it has been suggested, urged Kate to enrol into St. Andrews University when she heard that the future King of England was to study there. Supposedly, Carole Middleton never fails to encourage their friendship and tries very hard to make Kate acceptable to the royal family (Hughes). Suitable for the post-feminist era, ironically it are now the female relatives that incite their children to ensure a successful match.

Concerning family matters, this is not the only parallel between the Middleton and the Boleyn families. Both families are/were what is called nouveau-riche. Kate's parents are self-made middle class millionaires, and if Kate marries Prince William, interestingly she will become the second commoner to be Queen Consort after Anne Boleyn (Diebel). This is again underlines Anne Boleyn's extraordinariness. In an age, where class was determining the prospects of marriage, Anne overcame this great obstacle and married way above her degree. In that regard, this even allows for a comparison with a fairytale princess story like *Cinderella*.

Certainly, when establishing parallels between Kate Middleton and Anne Boleyn, it is unavoidable to look to another woman who was supposed to become Queen Consort of England one day: Lady Diana Spencer, Princess of Wales, another proclaimed fairy-tale princess. Dormer had no problems seeing Anne Boleyn as a contemporary stating that there are striking similarities between her character and Diana. She claims that Anne was the first consort of an English monarch to be extremely image-conscious, like Diana was. Anne Boleyn restructured the court aesthetically and made it plain that she was conveying sophistication, a particular 'je ne sais quoi' to the English court. Diana did the same thing with the court of the modern era, the media. Also, both Diana and Anne, as Dormer explains, were rather polarizing characters. On the one hand, they were unwaveringly supported by many people, but on the other hand, there were also a lot of people who criticised or even demonized them. This polarization is of course conflicting. On *The Tudors* it is shown what this does to Anne, whose polarizing nature eventually affects her own husband who first loves her passionately and then hates her passionately. And with regard to Lady Diana, the result of the excessive scrutiny of her person by the media due to both her polarizing effect and the fascination people had with her is well known (Paton and Gates).

The love triangle between Katherine, Henry and Anne, which is the main plot-line of the first two seasons of *The Tudors*, is in some ways similar to the love triangle between Lady Diana, Prince Charles and Camilla Parker-Bowles. This is even consciously alluded to by Hirst in some scenes of the programme, for instance in the scene when Anne finds out that Katherine still makes Henry's shirts (*Tud.* 2.1.29-32). Anne is furious with Henry for being so insensitive of having his still-wife performing household duties for him. For Anne, this is symbolic for their relationship. She exclaims: "They're not just shirts. They are you and me. They are you and her!". She tells Henry: "It's so hard, when we're to be married, but she is still here. You can't have three people in a marriage. Why can't you see that?". It has been recorded that Henry VIII. indeed still had his shirts mended by Katherine of Aragon when he was still in the middle of having his marriage to her annulled, and that Anne Boleyn became very angry about this (Lindsey 83). As many people will notice, Anne Boleyn's sentence in *The Tudors*: "you can't have three people in a marriage" is an intertextual reference to Lady Diana's statement in the famous BBC1 *Panorama* interview of the year 1995. Here, the reporter Martin Bashir asks the Princess of Wales: "Do you think that Ms. Parker-Bowles was a factor in the break-down of your marriage?", whereupon Diana answers: "Well, there were three of us in this marriage. So it was a bit crowded." This again demonstrates how the history of the Tudor dynasty is interpreted in contemporary terms. Hirst intentionally decided to use this little historical detail about Henry's shirts for a sequence in *The Tudors*, re-imagining it in association with contemporary figures. He says that he would never manipulate the facts to make parallels but that these parallels just occur (interviewed by Gomeshi). And these parallels can be interpreted in different ways. Hirst does not solely assign Anne Boleyn a parallel to Princess Diana but also to Katherine of Aragon. This happens in the exact same episode previously described. Anne's ascertainment that one cannot have three people in a marriage finally leads Henry to banish Katherine from court. As Katherine is leaving, many people have gathered to bid her farewell. They bow and issue their blessings to her. Amongst them his Thomas More who says to Katherine: "Blessed Lady. Queen of Hearts. There will be even greater crowds than these to welcome you when you return to London" (*Tud.* 2.1.45-48). Diana herself had coined the term 'Queen of Hearts' when asked by Bashir in the *Panorama* interview whether she thinks she would one day become Queen.

She responded that she would "like to be a queen of people's hearts, in people's hearts, but I don't see myself being Queen of that country." The media quickly picked up the term 'Queen of Hearts' ridiculing it during her life time. But after Diana's death, this designation was reinterpreted, recreated even, in public tributes, transcending its previous mockery. 'Queen of Hearts' evolved into 'Queen of All Our Hearts' with a different connotation. The term now embodied a hope for a closer relationship between the people and the royalty, Diana being symbolical for this new development (Brut 35-36). By using this with evident signification laden term, Hirst communicates a certain image, namely to show how popular Queen Katherine was with the people and that she liked the closeness to the people despite her royal status. With regards to Anne Boleyn, this phrase automatically demonstrates that she will not be admired by the people, since she is the reason for the 'Queen of Hearts' abandonment. Like Camilla Parker-Bowles, she will always be the other woman. Yet, at the same time, she also stands in line with Princess Diana, as the 'three people in a marriage' phrase has already demonstrated. Hirst constructs an image only to deconstruct it at a later point, so that it is still left open who is to take over which role in the love-triangles Katherine-Henry-Anne and Diana-Charles-Camilla.

At any rate, there are further similarities between Anne and Diana. Brian A. Pavlac argues that Anne Boleyn and Princess Diana were both disposable royal wives (and for that matter, so was Katherine of Aragon) as they were discarded when they were no longer needed by the monarchy. When Anne was unable to give Henry a son, he turned to another woman, Jane Seymour. Stigmatized by the everlasting annulment procedure with Katherine of Aragon, he knew that he needed to dispose of Anne in a different way, quicker and more conveniently. He let Cromwell conjure up a feigned trial against his wife that resulted in her execution. Diana's husband was not honourable either. Charles and Diana never were passionate lovers. Pavlac suggests that Prince Charles used Diana's virtuous status of virginity as the vital criteria for selecting her as his future wife. Interestingly, Charles had already been involved with Diana's sister who did not have the necessary virtuous reputation. This resembles the relationship that Henry VIII. had with Anne Boleyn's sister Mary. However, Charles had never desired Diana sexually and was still drawn to his old love Camilla. But Diana bore him two sons to secure the Windsor dynasty, thus fulfilling the job expected of her. Supposedly, their marriage was never a happy one. Charles maintained his affair with Camilla, and also Diana had extra-marital affairs with whose exposure in the media she embarrassed the monarchy. Finally, the monarchy agreed to a divorce in 1996. Unlike Anne's, Diana's life was spared but as Pavlac argues "the idea of the execution method has been resurrected with posthumous publications of Diana's alleged fear that she would be murdered to make way for Charles to legitimately remarry." So it was not surprising that her and her new partner Dodi Al-Fayed's sudden deaths in a car accident a year after the divorce has until now been subject to conspiracy theories. What if Charles wanted his ex-wife dead nonetheless, like Henry wanted Anne dead? One string of conspiracy theories of Diana's and Dodi Al-Fayed's death suspects the House of Windsor to have been the accident's originator out of religious reasons, as an Islamic match of the mother of the future King of England would cause horror. Emily Lomax claims that Diana in death, in terms of religion, race and international relations, is a figure of great importance, suggesting that she possibly has the potential to be designated an Islamic martyr *avant la lettre* (80-81). Posthumously, Anne Boleyn had also been declared a martyr by Protestant writers such as John Foxe. In his work *Actes and Monuments* or *Foxe's Book of Martyrs* he writes about Anne as "a zealous defender [...] of Christ's Gospel" who used her influential position as Queen of England for the "setting forth of sincere religion." Foxe also thinks that her condemnation to death was the result of "some secret practising of the papists" as she was "a mighty stop (...) to their purposes and proceedings." Furthermore, he believes that the successful reign of her daughter Elizabeth I. is proof of "the secret judgment of God in preserving and magnifying the fruit and offspring of that godly queen" (233-34). In that context, Anne Boleyn has also been referred to as a saint, as this passage of Foxe's book has the title "Oration to Saint Anne". After her death, Princess Diana had also been declared a saint by the media. It has been suggested that "somehow, Diana had paid, with her life and her suffering, for the desire of others" which is one of the reason why she is "always turned into a saint – a postmodern saint" (Richards, Wilson and Woodhead 1-3). Again, parallels between the Princess and the Queen cannot be dismissed.

In one scene of *The Tudors*, Queen Anne is shown leaving the church after a Maundy Thursday sermon, distributing alms to the poor and washing their feet (*Tud.* 2.8.8-10). One poor woman remarks that "this is twice as much as the old queen gave." Including such a scene, which is of no significance to the plot, is again helpful in constructing Anne Boleyn in sympathetic terms which (coincidentally?) points into Princess Diana's direction who has also been known for her charitable work with the poor and the sick. It is an old British custom, established by Edward III. in 1363, that a monarch gives out so-called Maundy Money to the poor and that he/she washes their feet commemorating Jesus who washed the disciples' feet after the Last Supper (*Time*, "Maundy Money"). Anne seems to take pleasure in performing this religious rite having no hesitations to kneel before a poor subject to wash their feet. This allows for a comparison to Princess Diana having no reservation to shake hands with people infected with the HI-Virus. Despite their royal statuses, these two women do not dread the contact to the poor and the suffering. Foxe praises Anne Boleyn for her charities and generosity expressing "how bountiful she was to the poor, passing not only the common example of other queens, but also the revenues almost of her estate" (233). Especially in her older years Anne devoted herself to charitable undertakings. She supported poor scholars providing money for their education, she gave out alms in the value of a hundred crowns and clothes to the poor on a weekly basis, she secretly financially helped widows and poor householders and every time she visited a village or town she would find out in advance if there were any needy families to make a monetary donation to them (Weir 280). In the series, her commitment to education is even taken as a catalyst for Cromwell's growing resentment towards Anne when she accuses him of having advised the King to use the resources gained by the dissolution of the monasteries for personal profit rather than using it for non-profit purposes (*Tud.* 2.9.8-10). The audience needs to be able to comprehend Cromwell's shifting attitude towards Anne from his fellow co-advocate of the Protestant cause to his objector that he gathers evidence against. Furious about the financial misuse (as well as that Cromwell has given his private lodgings at court to the Seymours), she threatens to destroy him which consequently gives Cromwell a motive for her own destruction. At any rate, however encompassing the actual Queen's benevolences were, they were hardly publicized during her time of life (Weir 280). This is a great contrast to Diana's charities whose every step was followed by the media.

A fact which undoubtedly joins the list of parallels between Diana Spencer and Anne Boleyn is of course their respective tragic deaths. Both died at the same age, if one emanates from Anne's earlier year of birth. Also, the incredible circumstances of their deaths call for fascination and a certain myth-making process. One royal wife is executed by her husband on trumped-up charges, the other one dies in a car accident in Paris after a chase with the paparazzi. Weir writes that after Anne's execution only few mourned her death. Nevertheless, a fortnight after her passing ballads spread all over in London which represented her as an utterly wronged heroine. With this, a legend was born which has persevered, with gathering impetus, ever since (337). If Anne had not died at the scaffold and Henry simply would have had her sent to a nunnery or to live in exile, her legendary status barely would have come into existence. Her early death, even though Anne Boleyn was middle-aged by Tudor standards when she died, incomprehensible in its nature now and then, created that myth. The same applies to Diana. Richards claims that Diana had, during her lifetime, been transformed to a global superstar and the aftermath of her passing had more similarities to that of a Hollywood star than a royal personage. For example, Hollywood stars Marilyn Monroe or Judy Garland both had tragic and troubled lives which were always publicized in the media. Their early deaths turned them into tragic heroines. The same happened with Diana. Jeffrey explains that when other popular people complete a normal life span, they simply fade away over the years. But 'stars' like Diana continue to live on in the popular memory. The early death becomes part of the legend (59-60). It is the tragedy and the malevolence of Anne's and Diana's respective fates that has fascinated and will keep on fascinating people.

It has already been mentioned that both Anne Boleyn and Diana Spencer were very image-conscious. And one aspect of this image-consciousness certainly is fashion. So, another designation that Diana and Anne share is that of the fashion-icon. In the beginning, Diana's style was very much controlled by the royal family but over the years Diana developed her own style of clothing. With the assistance of the renowned fashion commentator Colin McDowell and the then-chief editor of the British Vogue, Anna Harvey, she exchanged her puff-sleeved blouses and her 'Spencer-jackets' for popular designer labels like Versace and Manolo Blahnik. As demonstrated with Anne Boleyn's costumes in *The Tudors*, Diana's evolution concerning her way to dress was synchronized to the changes in her life. At first, Diana's style was classical, moderate and understated. Then, in the Nineties, she slowly began creating her own style which was elegant but unostentatious. It has even been suggested that the more she was dissociating herself from Charles, the better her taste of fashion became. Her growing self-confidence reflected itself in her clothing. As she had abandoned her marriage with the crown prince and had fought her eating disorder, the immaculateness of her sense of style reached its climax. The time from 1995 until her death were considered her most fashionable and elegant years. And according to the cliché that woman change their hairstyle when they change their life, Diana had her hair cut into the much copied 'Diana-bob'. Generally, her way of clothing became racier and her new sense of dress coined a new fashion trend which had been called 'Clean Chic' by the British *Vogue*. Every public, or even private, appearance of Diana were staged into her own little fashion show. Her dress would always be colour-coordinated with her shoes or handbag, as *The Tudors*' Anne Boleyn's costumes often harmonized with her headpieces or other accessories. From the shy kindergarten teacher, Diana had evolved into a figurehead of sense of style and trendiness. Not only became Gianni Versace her favourite designer, they also became close friends which contributed to her status as a fashion-icon *(FAZ)*.

In terms of modern-day celebrity, fashion is extremely important. Every year,

71

rankings of the one-hundred 'worst dressed' or 'best dressed' celebrities are published and reporters' first question on the red carpet is concerned with the designer label the star is wearing rather than their artistic accomplishment. So of course it is very convenient for *The Tudors*' producers to make use of this twentieth and twenty-first century phenomenon with the character of Anne Boleyn who was considered a fashion-icon of her time. At court, Anne dictated fashion unlike any other of Henry's queens. She took over tasteful French fashions and in France she was regarded as a woman with marvellous taste and of great inventiveness in terms of fashion, being referred to as "the glass of fashion." She introduced new styles, which were then imitated by the fashionable female courtiers, wearing them in a "gracefulness that rivalled venus" as a French courtier had observed (Weir 83, 150-51). Her image-consciousness closely connected to her obsession with fashion is an aspect that certainly translates well into the modern reinterpretation of her person in *The Tudors*. The chapter on her costumes and their variety has hopefully made this apparent. Her status as a Tudor fashion-icon, it can be suggested, might also have been responsible for the often very historically inaccurate reinterpretation of Anne Boleyn's clothing.

Be that as it may, on the whole, a certain similarity between Anne Boleyn and Diana Spencer cannot be denied. A concluding comparison of image 23 and image 24 stands to once more emphasize that aspect. Image 23 is a painting of Diana (unknown) sitting on the floor leaning her head, resting in her arm, on a white sofa. Image 24 shows Natalie Dormer as Anne Boleyn in promotional shot for *The Tudors* in an extremely similar pose. It can be argued that this photo of Dormer is possibly an intentional interpretation in terms of comparing Anne to Princess Diana. One could even go as far as to take the 1835 painting *Anne Boleyn in the Tower* (Edouard Cibot) in image 25 into consideration. The only difference to the two other images is that instead of leaning to a piece of furniture, as Diana and Natalie Dormer do, the sitter is crouched against her lady-in-waiting and her pose is mirror-inverted. The question now is which image is an interpretation of which image and whether all of that was done purposely, which is impossible to clearly define. Regardless of this question's answer, a parallel between the three pictures cannot be dismissed.

Certainly some of the offered parallels between Princess Diana and (*The Tudors'*) Anne Boleyn might seem far-fetched and of course this is all idle speculation. Yet, it is not entirely digressive to explore similarities between Diana and Anne in various contexts.

As Dormer's Anne Boleyn nevertheless is a fictional character reimagined in contemporary terms, it is worth comparing her to other fictional characters of the modern

72

television landscape. Keeping Anne Boleyn's portrayal as a fashion-conscious woman in the Showtime series in mind, a comparison to the central character of HBO's controversial show *Sex and the City*, Carrie Bradshaw (Sarah Jessica Parker), does not fall short. Dormer's Anne Boleyn somehow seems to combine the most defining characteristics of all the four female protagonists of the show. There is for instance Charlotte York's (Kristin Davis) constant mentioning of her desire to finally get married, the mental strength and intellectuality of Cynthia Nixon's character lawyer Miranda Hobbes and the seductiveness and sensuality of Samantha Jones (Kim Cattrall). Yet, it is the obsession with fashion of Carrie Bradshaw and her consequential status as a fashion icon that is the most remarkable aspect in the context of comparing *The Tudors*' Anne Boleyn to a fictional character of a television show set in the twentieth or twenty-first century. *Sex and the City* "views the battle of the sexes through the eyes of four explicitly Manhattan-dwelling women who laugh in the face of chastity (...), chain smoke, stalk next season's fashions with the ferocity of jungle cats and consider raw oysters and vodka stingers two of the major food groups" (Hass). The transtoriness of their romances can be compared to those of Henry and his (male) courtiers in *The Tudors*; the lavishness of the Tudor court is similar to the shows depiction of New York as centre of the world and its high society. In that world, fashion plays as much a role for Bradshaw as it does for Anne Boleyn in *The Tudors*. One scene of the show is particularly remarkable in this context: it is recorded that in early 1532 Henry VIII. spent a fortune on endowing Anne with a wardrobe worthy of a future Queen of England (Weir 232). This historical detail surely had to be deployed, although slightly altered, to represent Anne Boleyn as a fashion-conscious woman again. Right after Anne has been made Marquess of Pembroke, it is illustrated how she presents Henry the variety of her new luxurious gowns that she had made of the cloth that Henry had given to her. She asks whether he likes them and emphasizes that they are all made in the French fashion (*Tud.* 2.2.37-40). The way how Anne is thrilled with her new dresses is resembling to the way how Bradshaw acts after she comes home from a successful shopping spree carrying numerous bags containing designer fashion, proudly showing them off to her girlfriends. What is also striking is Anne's reference to France in the connection with fashion. France, especially its capital Paris, is one of the world's most important fashion strongholds. For the audience, this mention immediately implies what great significance fashion plays in Anne's life and that she is striving to always wear the newest, fashionable styles. The portrayal of columnist Carrie Bradshaw in that context is similar. She is very keen to experiment with her clothes. Her costumes often seem outrageous but admirable at the same time which has turned her into a fashion icon for many women. Carrie Bradshaw actress Parker is very closely connected to that status as the fact that in 2004 Parker was awarded with the 'Fashion Icon Award' for "her accomplished New Yorker style" proofs (*Stern*).

Two more minor stylistic details evoke a similar construction of Anne Boleyn as a Carrie Bradshaw of the sixteenth century, or for that matter, Carrie Bradshaw as an Anne Boleyn of the modern era. In the opening credits of *Sex and the City*, Bradshaw wears a light pink tutu dress. This dress is very similar to Anne's white ballet dress that she is wearing in the pageant when Henry notices her for the first time (see previous chapters). Also, where jewellery is concerned, Carrie and Anne display similar tastes. Although Carrie has no affinity for pompous crown-like headpieces, she shares Anne's preference to necklaces with pendants connected to her name. It has already been described that Anne Boleyn was often wearing necklaces with her initials. Carrie did not restrict herself to mere initials. For the most part of the show's season two and three, she is wearing the famous 'Carrie' necklace that, like the 'B' necklace can now, due to its cult status, be bought in other names.

A comparison between *Sex and the City* and *The Tudors* might seem incredible at first sight, but certain parallels in the reinterpretation of Anne Boleyn and the representation of Carrie Bradshaw and her attire seem unavoidable. This is again proof of the contemporary spirit that is merged into this historical television drama. Furthermore, the drawn parallels between Diana Spencer and Kate Middleton and Anne Boleyn help to see Henry's second wife as a contemporary. At the same time, this also suggests that history is always repetitive, as already been argued, and that even though conceptions of gender and sexuality are continuously evolving and changing, the root of the matter remains the same.

Conclusion

Without doubt, *The Tudors* has offered a portrayal of Anne Boleyn and Henry VIII. that had until then not yet existed. Due its serial format, *The Tudors* has allowed for a deeper, intenser reinterpretation of the Henrican court than could have been possibly realized in a two-hour film. Not only is *The Tudors* exceptional in its extensive illustration of Henry's life, and for that matter those of his six wives and his courtiers, it is also very exceptional concerning its contemporariness. Although the series depicts English sixteenth century history, it re-imagines it in modernized terms, as has been argued. This had been particularly noticeable where the portrayal of Henry's second wife Anne Boleyn was concerned. In his context, this thesis has attempted to analyse how Anne Boleyn is depicted in *The Tudors*, suggesting that the series re-imagined a very contemporary Anne Boleyn. For that matter, different aspects of her portrayal have been considered. For example, the comparison of promotional shots of Anne and Henry with modern-day fashion advertisements had the purpose to demonstrate how much embedded *The Tudors* is in popular understandings of beauty, alluding to the point that in order to make Anne Boleyn appealing to a mainstream audience she had to appear as a desirable, beautiful woman, with the result that the young, attractive actress Natalie Dormer was cast as Henry's second queen.

Another aspect of Anne's contemporariness was of course founded in the extensive portrayal of her personality. As typical of contemporary American television series, the stress is often more on character, as once the audience is captivated by the characters, they are willing to explore the events depicted. The construction of Anne in that regard was diversified and also changing within the course of the series. At first she was shown as a young woman who is unwillingly forced into Henry's arms by her male relatives, while at the same time she is had always been illustrated as virtuous and chaste, and as ideal female courtier. This shifted, however, with the second season, where it was increasingly revealed that Anne was indeed not as innocent as she had claimed to be. Another aspect under which Anne Boleyn was constructed was her representation as a key-reforming figure, whereas the depiction of her religiousness was very much adapted to modern standards, meaning that she was not portrayed in an religiously extreme way, as this would decrease her appeal to a post 9/11 American audience. On the whole, it has been argued that Dormer's Anne Boleyn has been portrayed in a rather sympathetic way, suggesting her as a victim of the male dominated Tudor world and as the tragic heroine of the *The Tudors'* first two seasons. This part of the thesis then concluded by arguing that the historical Anne Boleyn was a woman well ahead of her time who did not let herself be

75

restricted by the contemporary gender definitions. That is one of the reasons why she seems such a perfect character to realize on screen in our modern age.

The subsequent part of this thesis has then established the argument that Anne's contemporariness is furthermore manifested in her costumes, which of course greatly contributed to her visual re-imagination. Anne's costumes (as well as those of the series' other characters) had been an amalgam of sixteenths century clothes, often influenced by the Elizabethan Age rather than the Henrican Age, and modern-day fashion styles. In that context, it has also been proved that Anne's social rise is perceptible in the transformation of her dresses, whereas her costumes functioned as an helpful medium in consolidating the portrayal of her personality.

Then, with the objective to corroborate the previous argument that *The Tudors* offers a very modernized version of Anne Boleyn, both her historical and fictional character have been contrasted to modern-day women, both from the realm of reality and fiction. For that matter, it has for instance been argued that Hirst has given Dormer's Anne Boleyn lines that would immediately evoke an association with Princess Diana in order to show Anne as a contemporary. This final chapter also focused on Anne Boleyn's status as a fashion icon of the Tudor court, an aspect which translates well into our modern era. In order to prove this argument, Anne has been compared to *Sex and the City's* Carrie Bradshaw, the fashion queen of the twentieth/twenty-first century, and again to the image-consciousness of Princess Diana.

Certainly, the portrayal of Anne Boleyn in *The Tudors* is extremely influenced by the Zeitgeist of the twenty-first century. It is no surprise that the series has been lambasted by historians and critics for exactly that and its supposed historical inaccuracies. But I believe *The Tudors*, modernized and inaccurate as it sometimes may have been, has succeeded in something that history books, documentaries and two-hour films cannot do. Namely, to invest the re-imagined historical characters with such a multi-faceted personality that they truly no longer appear to be museum pieces, and in doing so, *The Tudors* manages to really "get to the heart of the story," as Henry had initially promised.

On June 20, 2010 the very last episode of *The Tudors* was aired in America, which has finished the series with the death of Henry. And although this thesis has only been concerned, due to its focus on Anne Boleyn, with the first and the second season, I would like to mention at this point, that the portrayal of his second wife has been the most intense and most significant compared to the depiction off all of his other five wives. Neither *The Tudors'* Katherine of Aragon nor Jane Seymour nor Anne of Cleves nor Katherine Howard nor Katherine Parr had been represented in the same extent and intensity. This might be

76

prove that Anne Boleyn is indeed the most fascinating and most important of Henry's wives, who accordingly deserves such a portrayal. And Dormer certainly left a mark in her portrayal of Henry's ill-fated queen. Only recently it has been announced in the press that she will soon appear on screen as yet another English queen, namely the young Queen Mother during the abdication crisis of Edward VIII. Astonishingly, this film will be produced by pop-singer and modern-day icon Madonna (Eden). So, in that respect, it will be interesting to see in how far this newest example of cinematic history will be influenced by contemporariness, as the Madonna-as-producer aspect already promises.

As been mentioned before, *The Tudors* have until now not received much attention from the academic realm. But I believe and hope that Michael Hirst's innovative historical television series will increasingly become the subject of academic research as there yet many aspects to explore for which it is certainly worth "to go back to the beginning."

Illustrations

Image 02: Hugo Boss
Advertisement

Image 01: Promotional
Shot Anne and Henry

Image 03: Promotional Shot Anne
and Henry

Image 04: Armani Advertisement
Victoria and David Beckham

Image 05: Portrait Anne Boleyn, Hever
Castle

Image 06: Portrait Anne Boleyn, National
Portrait Gallery London

Image 08:
Anne with
Diadem

Image 07: Anne, Field of
Cloth of Gold

Image 09: Anne with Coronet and
Purple Dress

Image 10: Anne at Hever Castle
(Hever Castle Dress)

Image 11: Anne
in Lady-in-Waiting
Dress

Image 12: Anne in White Virginal
Dress, with Henry

Image 13: Anne at Pageant with Henry

Image 14: First Scene of
Anne, in France

Image 16: Anne's Execution

Image 15: Anne, Queen of England

Image 17: Gothic,
Transparent Dress

Image 18: Sleeveless Dress

Image 19: Dress with Slit
Bodice, during Christmas

Image 20: Queen Katherine
of Aragon

Image 21: Servant Anne

Image 22: Katherine
Banished From Court

Image 23: Princess Diana

Image 24: Promotional Shot
Anne

Image 25: Painting Anne Boleyn in the Tower
(E. Cibot)

Bibliography

Baldassare Castiglione. *The Book of the Courtier.* Trans. Charles S. Singleton. Garden
  City, NY: Doubleday, 1959.

Brut, Rosalind. "Princess Diana: A Sign of the Times." *Diana, the Making of a Media Saint.*
  Ed. Jeffrey Richards, Scott Wilson and Linda Woodhead. London: I.B. Tauris, 1999.
  20-39.

Devoucoux, Daniel. *Mode im Film: Zur Kulturanthropologie Zweier Medien.* Bielefeld:
  Transcript, 2007.

Engelmann, Felicia. "Gute Zeiten, Schlechte Zeiten: In der TV-Serie *Die Tudors* Ist
  Geschichte eine Soap-Opera." *P.M. History* Mar. 2010: 41.

Foxe, John. "Oration to Saint Anne Boleyn." Vol. 5 of *The Acts and Monuments of John
  Foxe; With a Life of the Martyrologist, and Vindication of the Work.* Ed. George Townsend.
  10 vols. New York: AMS Press, 1965. 232-234.

Hirst, Michael. Foreword. *The Tudors: It's Good to Be King.* By Michael Hirst and Michael
  Wilder. New York: Simon Spotlight, 2007. xi-xvii.

Hirst, Michael, writ. *The Tudors: Seasons 1 & 2.* Dir. Ciaran Donnelly et al. Perf. Natalie
  Dormer, Jonathan Ryhs Meyers, et al. DVD. Sony Pictures, 2008.

Ives, Eric. *The Life and Death of Anne Boleyn.* Oxford et al.: Blackwell, 2004.

Krontiris, Tina. *Oppositional Voices: Women as Writers and Translators of Literature in the
  English Renaissance.* London et al.: Routledge, 1992.

Luhrmann, Baz. *Romeo and Juliet.* Perf. Claire Danes and Leonardo DiCaprio. DVD.
  Twentieth Century Fox, 2002.

Lindsey, Karen. *Divorced, Beheaded, Survived: A Feminist Reinterpretation of the Wives of
  Henry VIII.* Cambridge, MA: Da Capo Press, 1995.

Lomax, Emily. "Diana Al-Fayed: Ethic Marketing and the End(s) of Racism." Ed. Jeffrey
  Richards, Scott Wilson and Linda Woodhead. London: I.B. Tauris, 1999. 74-97.

Lucie-Smith, Edward. *Furniture – A Concise History.* London:Thames and Hudson, 1979.

Mikhaila, Ninya and Jane Malcolm-Davies. *The Tudor Tailor: Reconstructing
  16-th Century Dress.* London: Batsford, 2006.

Richards, Jeffrey. "The Hollywoodisation of Diana." *Diana, the Making of a Media Saint.*
  Ed. Jeffrey Richards, Scott Wilson and Linda Woodhead. London: I.B. Tauris, 1999.
  59-73.

Richards, Jeffrey, Scott Wilson, and Linda Woodhead. "Introduction: Saint Diana." Ed.
  Jeffrey Richards, Scott Wilson, and Linda Woodhead. London: I.B. Tauris, 1999.
  74-97. 1-19.

Richardson, Glenn. "*Anne of the Thousand Days.*" *Tudors and Stuarts on Film.* Ed. Susan
Doran and Thomas S. Freeman. Basingstoke: Palgrave Macmillan, 2009. 60-75.

Rosenstone, Robert A. *History on Film / Film on History,* Harlow, et al.: Pearson
Education, 2006.

Sanders, Julie. *Adaptation and Appropriation,* New York, et al.: Routledge, 2006.

Semenza, Greg Colón. "Introduction: An Age for All Time." *The English Renaissance in
Popular Culture: An Age for All Time.* Ed. Greg Colón Semenza. New York:
Palgrave Macmillan, 2010. 1-21.

Toplin, Robert Brent. *Reel History: In Defense of Hollywood.* Lawrence, Can.: UP of
Kansas, 2002.

Weir, Alison. *The Six Wives of Henry VIII.* New York: Grove Press, 1991.

Wray, Ramona. "Henry's Desperate Housewives: *The Tudors,* the Politics of
Historiography, and the Beautiful Body of Jonathan Rhys Meyers." *The
English Renaissance in Popular Culture: An Age for All Time.* Ed. Greg Colón
Semenza. New York: Palgrave Macmillan, 2010. 25-42.

Electronic Sources

Armstrong, Stephen. "She Won't Lose Her Head." *The Sunday Times* 23 Sept. 2007.15
Mar. 2010 <http://entertainment.timesonline.co.uk/tolarts_and_entertainment/
tv_and_radio/article2499952.ece>.

Bergin, Joan. "The Royal Stylemakers Part 1." *Showtime Offical Site* 20 May 2007. 27 Jan.
2010 <http://www.sho.com/site/video/brightcove/series/title.do?bcpid=
14034154001&bclid=1340048700&bctid=1311281440>.

Bergin, Joan. "The Royal Stylemakers Part 3." *Showtime Offical Site* 20 May 2007. 27 Jan.
2010 <http://www.sho.com/site/video/brightcove/series/title.do?bcpid=
14034154001&bclid=1340048700&bctid=1311281438>.

Bergin, Joan. "The Tudor Costumes: Anne Boleyn." *The Tudors Wiki* 24 June 2010. 30
June 2010 <http://tudorswiki.sho.com/page/The+Tudors+Costumes+Anne+Boleyn>.

Bianco, Robert. "Henry Rocks, Heads Roll on Richer, Lustier *Tudors.*" *USA Today* 28 Mar.
2008. 5 Feb. 2010 <http://www.usatoday.com/life/ television/reviews/2008-03-27-
tudors-season-2_N.htm>.

Brook Sally. "Who is the Real Kate Middleton?." *The Sun* 28 July 2007. 26 June 2010
<http://www.thesun.co.uk/sol/homepage/news/250554/Who-is-the-real-Kate-
Middleton.html>.

Deacon, Michael. "King of the Swingers." *The Daily Telegraph* 29 Sept 2007. 25 Feb. 2010
 <http://www.telegraph.co.uk/culture/tvandradio/3668250/King-of-the-swingers.html>.

Diebel, Frank Heinz. "Hat Kate Middleton Angst vor der Krone?." *Die Welt* 5 Oct. 2007. 24
 June 2010 <http://www.welt.de/vermischtes/article1237415/ Hat_Kate_Middleton_
 Angst_vor_der_Krone.html>.

Dormer, Natalie. Interview. "Season 2 Podcast: Natalie Dormer." *Showtime Official
 Site* 2 Apr. 2008. 27 Jan.2010 <http://www.sho.com/site/video/brightcove/series/
 title.dobcpid=14034154001&bclid=1540979063&bctid=1568084904>.

"Drunken Jonathan Rhys Meyers Launches Foul-Mouthed Tirade at Airport Staff After He's
 Banned from Boarding Plane." *The Daily Mail* 18 May 2010. 22 May 2010
 <http://www.dailymail.co.uk/tvshowbiz/article-1279301/Drunken-Jonathan-Rhys-
 Meyers-launches-foul-mouthed-tirade-airport- staff-hes-banned-boarding-
 plane.html>.

Eden, Richard. "Madonna Casts Natalie Dormer to Portray the 'Game-Playing'
 Queen Mother." *The Daily Telegraph* 3 July 2010. 17 July 2010
 <http://www.telegraph.co.uk/news/newstopics/celebritynews/madonna/
 7870311/Madonna-casts-Natalie-Dormer-to-portray-the-game-playing-Queen-
 Mother.html>.

Elias, Justine Elias. "Buffy Is Sweet, 16 and Slaying Vampires." *The New York Times* 27
 Apr. 2007. 13 May 2010 <http://www.nytimes.com/1997/04/27/tv/buffy-is-sweet-16-
 and-slaying-vampires.html?scp=1&sq=buffy%20sweet%2016&st=cse>.

"Foreign News: Maundy Money." *Time* 4 Apr. 1932. 4 June 2010
 <http://www.time.com/time/magazine/article/0,9171,743446,00.htm>.

Fletcher, Bruce. "Why The Tudors Is Hilarious Historical Bunk:" *The Telegraph* 1 Aug 2008.
 11 May 2010 <http://www.telegraph.co.uk/culture/tvandradio/3557583/Why-The-
 Tudors-is-hilarious-historical-bunk.html>.

Gates, Anita. "The Royal Life (Some Facts Altered)." *The New York Times* 23 Mar. 2008.
 13 May 2010 <http://www.nytimes.com/2008/03/23/arts/television/23gate.htm>.

Hass, Nancy. "'Sex' Sells, in the City and Elsewhere." *The New York Times* 11 July 1999.
 2 July 2010 <http://query.nytimes.com/search/sitesearch?query=Sex'+Sells,
 +in+the+City+and+Elsewhere&srchst=cse>.

"Henry VIII 500th Anniversary Events." *Tudorhistory.org*. 6 Dec. 2009. 15 May 2010
 <http://tudorhistory.org/files/henry500.html >.

"Henry VIII 2009 Events." *Facebook*. 2 Mar. 2009. 14 Apr. 2010
    <http://www.facebook.com/pages/Henry-VIII-2009-Events/60403115796>.

Herrup, Cynthia. "The Hot Dynasty: The Tudors on Film and TV." *American Historical*
    Association 30 Sept. 2009. 27 Feb. 2010 <http://www.historians.org/perspectives/
    issues/2009/0904/0904fil2.cfm>.

"Hidden Meanings on The Tudors: Falcon/Hawk." *The Tudors Wiki* 29 June 2010. 11 July
    2010 <http://tudorswiki.sho.com/page/HIDDEN+MEANINGS+on+the+Tudors>.

Hirst, Michael. Interview. "Season 2 Podcast: Michael Hirst Part 1." *Showtime Official Site*
    2 Apr. 2008. 26 Jan. 2010 <http://www.sho.com/site/video/brightcove/series/
    title.do?bcpid=14034154001&bclid=1540979063&bctid =1579853736>.

Hirst, Michael. Interview with Jian Gomeshi. "lian Gomeshi Interviews Screenwriter
    Michael About the Return of *The Tudors*." *CBC Radio* 30 Sept. 2008. 12 Feb. 2010
    <http://www.cbc.ca/wordsatlarge/blog/2008/09/as_season_two_of_the_tudors_be.
    html>.

Hohenadel, Kristin. "He's Henry the Eighth, He Is." *The Sunday Times* 8 Apr. 2007. 11 Apr.
    2010 <http://entertainment.timesonline.co.uk/tol/arts_and_entertainment/
    tv_and_radio/article1613666.ece >.

Holden, Stephen. "*10 Things I Hate About You* (1999) Film Review: It's Like You Know,
    Sonnets And Stuff" *The New York Times* 31 Mar 1999. 15 May 2010
    <http://movies.nytimes.com/movie/review?res=9501e7db1f30f932a05750c
    0a96f958260>.

Hughes, Mark. "When Mother Knows Best."*The Independent* 24 Mar. 2008. 25 June 2010
    <http://www.independent.co.uk/news/people/profiles/when-mother-knows-best-
    799871.html>.

Irvine, Chris. "Henry Will Not Get Fat in Historically Inaccurate *The Tudors*." *The*
    Daily Telegraph 31 Aug. 2008. 4 Feb. 2010 <http://www.telegraph.co.uk/news/
    newstopics/celebritynews/2655240/ Henry-VIII-will-not-get-fat-in-historically-
    inaccurate-The-Tudors.html>.

James, Caryn. "Televison Review: All the President's Quips: Levity at the White House.
    The New York Times 22 Sept. 1999. 2 July 2010 <http://query.nytimes.com/ search/
    television?query=All+the+President's+Quips:&x=0&y=0>.

James, Caryn. "TV Weekend: No Horse Heads, But Plenty of Prozac – *The Sopranos*."
    The New York Times 8 Jan.1999. 2 July 2010 <http://www.nytimes.com/1999/01/
    08/movies/tv-weekend-no-horse- heads-but-plenty-of-prozac.html>.

La Ferla, Ruth. "Tudormania." *The New York Times* Mar. 16 2009. 2 Feb. 2010
    <http://www.nytimes.com/2009/03/16/fashion/16TRENDS.html?_r=1&scp
    =1&sq=tudormania&st=cse>

Leith, William. "Last Night's TV." *The Guardian* 30 Aug. 2008. 4 Feb. 2010
    <http://www.guardian.co.uk/culture/2008/aug/30/television.television2>.

IMDb.com. 1990. The Internet Movie Database. 11 Feb. 2010 <http://www.imdb.com>.

Martin, Nicole. "BBC Period Drama *The Tudors* is 'Gratiously Awful' Says Dr. David
    Starkey." *The Daily Telegraph* 16 Oct. 2008. 4 Feb 2010
    <http://www.telegraph.co.uk/news/newstopics/celebritynews/3210142/
    BBC-period-drama-The-Tudors-is-gratuitously-awful-says-Dr-David-Starkey.html>.

O'Toole, Lesley. "Rachel Bilson: She's The One." *The Independent* 31 Oct. 2006. 1 June
    2010 <http://www.independent.co.uk/news/people/profiles/ rachel-bilson-shes-the-
    one-422345.html>.

Paton, Maureen. "Boho Boleyn Girl: Actress Natalie Dormer." *The Dailymail* 7 Nov. 2008.
    11 Mar. 2010 <http://www.dailymail.co.uk/home/you/article-1081189/Boho-Boleyn-
    girl-Actress-Natalie-Dormer.html>.

Pavlac, Brian A. "Parallels of Anne Boleyn and Princess Di: Disposable Royal Wives." *Prof.
    Pavlac's Women's History Resource Site: Anne Boleyn* 29 Mar 2007. 22 June 2010
    <http://departments.kings.edu/womens_history/anneboleyn.html#prindi>.

"Prinzessin Diana und Grace Kelly: Unvergessen, Unvergleichlich, Vergleichbar." *FAZ* 31
    Aug. 2007. 7 July 2010 <http://www.faz.net/s/RubB62D23B6C6964CC9ABBFCB78
    BC047A8D/Doc~EE0AA036CECA34263A1625349C491674F~ATpl~Ecommon~Sc
    ontent.html>.

Rochlin, Mary. "Joan Bergin: *The Tudors*." *The New York Times*, 7 June 2009. 20 Feb.
    2009 <http://www.nytimes.com/2009/06/07/arts/television/07berg.html?
    _r=1&scp=1&sq=joan%20bergin&st=cse>.

"Sarah Jessica Parker Wird zur Mode-Ikone Gekürt." *Der Stern* 2 Apr 2004. 10 July 2010
    <http://www.stern.de/lifestyle/mode/fashion-icon-award-sarah-jessica-parker-wird-
    zur-mode-ikone-gekuert-522271.html >.

Sessions, David. "Henry Fussy." *Patrol* 7 Apr. 2008. 16 May 2010
    <http://www.patrolmag.com/arts/361/henry-fussy>.

Sherwin, Adam. "Bloated Henry Transformed into a Slim, Young Lady Killer. "*The Times*
    21 Apr. 2007. 22 June 2010 <http://entertainment.timesonline.co.uk/ tol/
    arts_and_entertainment/tv_and_radio/article1680656.ece >.

"Spekulationen um Verlobung von Prinz William and Kate Middleton." *Krone* 21. June
2010. 27 June 2010 <http://www.krone.at/Show-Stars/Spekulationen_um_
Verlobung_von_Prinz_William_und_Kate-Prinz_William_ist_28-Story-206044>.

Spencer, Diana. Interview with Martin Bashir. *Panorama Interview*. BBC1. Nov.1995. 9
May 2010 <http://www.bbc.co.uk/politics97/diana/ panorama.html>.

Strachan, Alex. "Dormer Embodies – and Disembodies – Anne Boleyn." *National Post* 17
Oct 2008. 13 Feb. 2010 <http://www.nationalpost.com/ news/story.html?id=
fd1ae810-8723-4a62-a07a-9eb5ccddfcf3>.

"Ten Greatest Britons Chosen." *BBC News: Entertainment* 20 Oct. 2002. 4 Apr. 2010
<http://news.bbc.co.uk/2/hi/entertainment/2341661.stm>.

"*The Tudors* – Costume Designer Joan Bergin." *Television New Zealand* 29 May 2007. 2
June 2010 <http://tvnz.co.nz/content/1636878 >.

"Tudor Costumes: Women's Dress: The Atifet." *The Tudors Wiki* 10 Apr. 2010. 11 May
2010 <http://tudorswiki.sho.com/page/The+Tudors+Costumes+Women's+Dress>.

"Tudors in Movies and on Television." *Tudorhistory.org.* 25 Apr. 2010. 15 May 2010
<http://tudorhistory.org/movies/ >.

"When Royals Became Rock Stars." *Time* 22 Mar. 2007. 4 Feb. 2010
<http://www.time.com/time/magazine/article/0,9171,1601865,00.html>.

Wordsworth, Arminata. "Britain's Modern Couple."*National Post* 23. June 2010. 27 June
2010 <http://www.nationalpost.com/news/canada/Britain+modern+couple/3188472/
story.html >.

Register of Illustrations

Image 01:   "The Tudor Costumes: Anne Boleyn – S2 Pt1." *Season Two Promo Shot. The Tudors Wiki*. 05 May 2010. 19 May 2010 <http://tudorswiki.sho.com/page/The+Tudors+Costumes:+Anne+Boleyn+-+S2+pt1>.

Image 02:   Testino, Mario. *Hugo Boss Mainline (Spring/Summer 2008). Photobucket.* 12 May 2010 <http://photobucket.com/images/hugo%20boss%20ad/ >.

Image 03:   "Season 2 Promo Pic." *The Tudorswiki* 8 Mar. 2009. 13 May 2010 <http://tudorswiki.sho.com/photos/album/88691/season+2+Promo+pic+album/photo/4362488/Season+2+promo+pic>.

Image 04:   Alas, Mert and Marcus Piggott. *Emporio Armani Campaign (Fall 2009).* 13 May 2010 <http://www.whyfame.com/gossip/david_ and_ victoria_beckham _in_armani_ads_10983>.

Image 05:   *Anne Boleyn.*1534. Hever Castle, Kent. *Wikipedia* 30 May 2006. 17 May 2010 <http://en.wikipedia.org/wiki/File:Anneboleyn2.jpg>.

Image 06:   *Anne Boleyn.* 1533-1536. National Portrait Gallery, London. 17 May 2010 <http://www.npg.org.uk/collections/search/portrait.php?search=ap&npgno=668>.

Image 07:   "The Tudor Costumes: Anne Boleyn." *The Tudors Wiki* 24 Apr. 2010. 22 May 2010 <http://tudorswiki.sho.com/page/The+Tudors+Costumes+:+Anne+Boleyn>.

Image 08:   "Tudor Costumes: Women's Dress: Diadems." *The Tudors Wiki* 10 Apr. 2010. 19 May 2010 <http://tudorswiki.sho.com/page/The+Tudors+Costumes+:+Women's+Dres

Image 09:   "The Tudor Costumes: Anne Boleyn." *The Tudors Wiki* 24 Apr. 2010. 22 May 2010 <http://tudorswiki.sho.com/page/The+Tudors+Costumes+Anne+Boleyn>.

Image 10:   "The Tudor Costumes: Anne Boleyn." *The Tudors Wiki* 24 Apr. 2010. 23 May 2010 <http://tudorswiki.sho.com/page/The+Tudors+Costumes+:+Anne+Boleyn>.

Image 11:   "The Tudor Costumes: Anne Boleyn." *The Tudors Wiki* 24 Apr. 2010. 25 May 2010 <http://tudorswiki.sho.com/page/The+Tudors+Costumes+:+Anne+Boleyn>.

Image 12:   "The Tudor Costumes: Anne Boleyn." *The Tudors Wiki* 24 Apr. 2010. 16 May
             2010
             <http://tudorswiki.sho.com/page/The+Tudors+Costumes+:+Anne+Boleyn>.

Image 13:   "The Tudor Costumes: Anne Boleyn." *The Tudors Wiki* 24 Apr. 2010. 21 May
             2010
             <http://tudorswiki.sho.com/page/The+Tudors+Costumes+:+Anne+Boleyn>.

Image 14:   "The Tudor Costumes: Anne Boleyn." *The Tudors Wiki* 24 Apr. 2010. 16 May
             2010
             <http://tudorswiki.sho.com/page/The+Tudors+Costumes+:+Anne+Boleyn>.

Image 15:   "The Tudor Costumes: Anne Boleyn – S2 Pt1." *The Tudors Wiki.* 05 May
             2010. 15 May 2010 <http://tudorswiki.sho.com/page/The+Tudors+Costumes:
             +Anne+Boleyn+-+S2+pt1>.

Image 16:   "The Tudor Costumes: Anne Boleyn – S2 Pt2." *The Tudors Wiki.* 28 Apr.
             2010. 30 May 2010 <http://tudorswiki.sho.com/page/The+Tudors+Costumes:
             +Anne+Boleyn+-+S2+pt2+%26+S4>.

Image 17:   "The Tudor Costumes: Anne Boleyn – S2 Pt1." *The Tudors Wiki.* 05 May
             2010. 19 May 2010 <http://tudorswiki.sho.com/page/The+Tudors+Costumes:
             +Anne+Boleyn+-+S2+pt1>.

Image 18:   "The Tudor Costumes: Anne Boleyn – S2 Pt2." *The Tudors Wiki* 28 Apr. 2010.
             31 May 2010 <http://tudorswiki.sho.com/page/The+Tudors+Costumes:
             +Anne+Boleyn+-+S2+pt2+%26+S4>.

Image 19:   "The Tudor Costumes: Anne Boleyn – S2 Pt2." *The Tudors Wiki* 28 Apr. 2010.
             25 May 2010 <http://tudorswiki.sho.com/page/The+Tudors+Costumes:
             +Anne+Boleyn+-+S2+pt2+%26+S4>.

Image 20:   "The Tudor Costumes: Katherine of Aragon." *The Tudors Wiki* 3 May 2010. 11
             June 2010 <http://tudorswiki.sho.com/page/The+Tudors+Costumes+:
             +Katherine+of+Aragon>.

Image 21:   "The Tudor Costumes: Anne Boleyn." *The Tudors Wiki* 24 Apr.
             2010. 28 May 2010 <http://tudorswiki.sho.com/page/ The+Tudors+
             Costumes+:+Anne+Boleyn>.

Image 22:   "The Tudor Costumes: Katherine of Aragon." *The Tudors Wiki* 3 May 2010.
             12 June 2010 <http://tudorswiki.sho.com/page/The+Tudors+Costumes+:
             +Katherine+of+Aragon>.

Image 23:   "Blog." *Princess Diana Remembered* 27 Mar. 2008. 27 June 2010
            <http://diana-remembered.spaces.live.com/blog/cns!2244878A8C9
            B75DA!1828.entry>.

Image 24:   "The Tudor Costumes: Anne Boleyn – S2 Pt1." *Season Two Promo Shot. The
            Tudors Wiki.* 05 May 2010. 11 June 2010 <http://tudorswiki.sho.com/page/
            The+Tudors+Costumes:+Anne+Boleyn+-+S2+pt1>.

Image 25:   Cibot, Eduard. *Anne Boleyn in the Tower.*1835. Musée Rolin, Autun. 11 June
            2010 <http://www.musees-bourgogne.org/les_musees/musees_bourgogne_
            gallerie.php?lg=fr&id=69&theme=archeologie&id_ville=&id_gallerie=45352#h
            aut>.

Printed in Great Britain
by Amazon